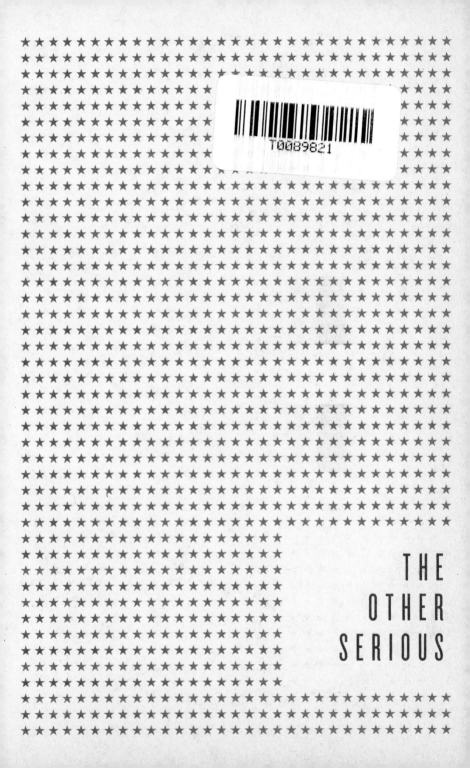

T0089821

THE
OTHER
SERIOUS

ESSAYS FOR THE NEW
AMERICAN GENERATION

THE

OTHER

SERIOUS

HARPER ● PERENNIAL

NEW YORK • LONDON • TORONTO • SYDNEY • NEW DELHI • AUCKLAND

CHRISTY WAMPOLE

HARPER ● PERENNIAL

A hardcover edition of this book was published in 2015 by HarperCollins Publishers.

HarperCollins books may be purchased for educational, business, or sales promotional use. For information please e-mail the Special Markets Department at SPsales@harpercollins.com.

FIRST HARPER PERENNIAL EDITION PUBLISHED 2016.

Designed by William Ruoto

The Library of Congress has catalogued the hardcover edition as follows:
Wampole, Christy
  [Essays. Selections]
  The other serious : essays for the new American generation / Christy Wampole.—
First edition.
    pages cm
  ISBN 978-0-06-232035-3 (hardback)—ISBN 978-0-06-232036-0 (trade pb)—ISBN 978-0-06-232037-7 (e-book) 1. United States—Civilization—21st century. 2. Social values—United States—History—21st century. 3. United States—Social conditions—21st century. I. Title. II. Title: Essays for the new American generation.
  E169.12W345 2015
  973.93—dc23
                                   2014042027

16 17 18 19 20   OV/RRD   10 9 8 7 6 5 4 3 2 1

In memory of my grandpa

Contents

Introduction: A Heavy Life or a Light One 1

The Glare of the Enlightenment 5

The Great American Irony Binge 27

The Patina of Things 65

On Distraction 71

The Emotive Spectacle 101

Intergenerational Conversation 105

Toward a Sterile Future 125

Southern Niceness 149

On Awkwardness 165

Treat Your Country Like Your Child, Not Your Parent 183

The Metaphor of Masking Tape 185

You Have No Power over Me 189

The Bad Serious 203

The Other Serious 211

Postscript: The Lightness of the Ladybug 237

The Generations pouring
From times of endless date,
In their going, in their flowing
Ever form the steadfast State;
And Humanity is growing
Toward the fullness of her fate.

—AN EXCERPT FROM
  HERMAN MELVILLE'S "A Canticle"

THE
OTHER
SERIOUS

Introduction: A Heavy Life or a Light One

The heavier the burden, the closer our lives come to the earth, the more real and truthful they become. Conversely, the absolute absence of a burden causes man to be lighter than air, to soar into heights, take leave of the earth and his earthly being, and become only half real, his movements as free as they are insignificant. What then shall we choose? Weight or lightness?

—MILAN KUNDERA, *The Unbearable Lightness of Being*

Essays are barometers of the intellect. We are all atmospheric creatures, influenced by the cultural weather around us; the essayist takes it as her role to say something about the way the atmosphere plays upon a person and exerts pressure on the mind and its bearing. What causes the spirit to slump? What lifts it? The constant flux between lightness and heaviness is the basic biographical flux of human life. Essays gauge this flux but also respond to it by pressing back, meeting experience with an equal exertion.

This collection offers a map of the high- and low-pressure systems of American culture and its effects on the author's brain. Since the turn of the new millennium, various fronts have pushed their way across the continent, some as thin as cirrus wisps and others thickly cumulus, shaping the unstable meteorological profile of life in the States. From whatever altitude you experience these weatherlike events, you understand that heaviness or lightness produces effects on the psyche of each individual, caught in a low trough or evaporated upward toward the stratosphere. We are subject to cultural weather and weathering. We can never really be free of these pressure systems.

A first problem: is it possible to write weightfully about light things? In other words, if one's subject is superficial, does the writing that describes it risk an equal superficiality? This is the problem with the greater part of contemporary writing: the material it has at hand is so flimsy, the words stay suspended in midair, saying nearly nothing. The writer has little leverage in an atmosphere without gravity. My attempt here is to use the essay—a light form by nature—to give a little more mass to the parts of culture that might need it. Paradoxically, the essay's open, accommodating nature leaves a vacancy that can be filled with what is heavily relevant. Strangely, the heavy is accessed through a lightness of form. I don't believe I'm alone in my impulse to add a good kind of weight to my lived experience. In fact, I think this is a central problem for many Americans who have the consciousness to notice it. Life feels too light. Despite those difficult aspects of our economy and our politics that press people down, there is a distinct flimsiness to many aspects of contemporary American culture. The burdens of an increasingly complicated life encumber almost everyone, which means that our only experience with weight is a negative one. But it is possible to ask for and receive a substantial and meaningful heaviness through a certain kind of thinking and writing and making. The structures that used to provide a comforting weight have all caved in. These include the big ideas and ideologies that for centuries worked provisionally for some but to the detriment of many. People born after their collapse probably never even experienced the sensation of sureness you feel when you hold a solid thing in your hand. I wrote these essays mainly for them. I push a single idea: we are free to pick the thickness of our experiences.

It is time to get serious. Joyfully serious.

The kind of seriousness I describe in the following pages—mostly implicitly but very explicitly toward the end—works as both an anchor and a buoy. The turn in the late twentieth century toward ironic buoyancy had a certain refreshing novelty that felt good for a change. It helped us out of our helplessness in the face of the seemingly unavoidable repetition of history's mistakes. But its virtues were only provisional. If people feel empty despite the fullness of life—the fullness of plates, schedules, and bank accounts—it is because we bob between two tendencies: the lightness of paper irony and the heaviness of leaden politics. Neither satisfies. Someone who is very young, who didn't witness the transition that led to this strange state of affairs, might not see the problem with a life of busyness, empty chatter, and disposable experiences. They certainly wouldn't prefer what they see there in the distance, the person drowning from an inability to let go of the dense dogma they cling to. An alternative: a kind of seriousness that is more than willing to accept a certain measure of gravity but that refuses to go all the way down.

To be joyfully serious is to resist some of the American myths we rely on. The fetishizing of happiness, for example, turns everything into a brittle, surface satisfaction. The emphasis on getting happy—or, at minimum, performing happiness—makes life into a scramble for what you can accumulate. This book has nothing to do with superficial happiness, with getting, or with spending. It is about how to add consequence to consciousness. These essays also resist the American myth of fulfillment through material gain. Only your mind and your will are needed to undermine the false belief that things or entertainments can bring lasting satisfaction. Countless ideas invite us at every second to think about them; it is a simple question of accepting their invitation.

This book urges clemency for seriousness, but a special kind. While the throwaway logic of total irony has left us blank and the autocratic logic of dogmatism has blacked out some of our best pages, we have other capacities for writing, thinking, and acting in a way that opens rather than forecloses possibilities. You'll find in the following pages a variety of thought experiments, tableaux, portraits, meditations, memories, predictions, and calls to action. The weight of this collection varies from essay to essay. Some are compact, others less so. Some are fragmented, skipping across the surface like flat stones, while others sink down deeply in the ideas. But the same spirit of joyful seriousness is described and acted out in each one.

A good essay asks the reader to continue its work after the final sentence. I hope these essays have enough goodness for their work to go further.

The Glare of the Enlightenment

There is strong shadow where there is much light.

—GOETHE, *Götz von Berlichingen*

America exists by virtue of its brilliant explosions. It's right there in the national anthem, in plain sight: "And the rockets' red glare, the bombs bursting in air, / Gave proof through the night that our flag was still there." Without the pyrotechnic spectacle, the symbol of our nation would be invisible. We're like the moon, our lunar cousin, who'd remain unseen in shallow space without the sun's nuclear incandescence.

The text of the American national anthem is beautiful,

all patriotism and politics aside. It has an ekphrastic quality; that is, it turns a thing—the flag—into an object of aesthetic contemplation. In this brief excerpt, the first stanza of a longer poem, Francis Scott Key sets a simple scene: the American flag survives a British bombardment in the War of 1812. By implicit extension, America survives the onslaught of its enemy. The verses evoke an unsure atmosphere in which the flag works as *evidence* (the Latin root *videre* means "to see") of the nation's durability. "The Star-Spangled Banner," like America itself, is visual in nature. Look at it. It wants you to see:

> *Oh, say, can you see, by the dawn's early light,*
> *What so proudly we hailed at the twilight's last gleaming?*
> *Whose broad stripes and bright stars, through the perilous*
>   *fight,*
> *O'er the ramparts we watched, were so gallantly*
>   *streaming?*
> *And the rockets' red glare, the bombs bursting in air,*
> *Gave proof through the night that our flag was still there.*
> *Oh, say, does that star-spangled banner yet wave*
> *O'er the land of the free and the home of the brave?*

The "rockets' red glare" verse is the only statement in the song; the rest is composed of questions. Ours is an interrogative anthem. Once you notice the eye's importance in the national song, you see its compatibility with our culture of looking. Really stare at these words: "can you see," "dawn's early light," "twilight's last gleaming," "bright stars," "we watched," "rockets' red glare," "star-spangled" (the word "spangle" means a small glittering piece of metal). The lights that shine in the poem are either celestial (dawn, twilight, stars) or martial (rockets, bombs). This connection between war and the heavens is everywhere in military history: Blue Angels, Desert Storm, Kamikaze (meaning divine wind or spirit wind), and Blitzkrieg (lightning war). The word "explode" and the word "applause" share the Latin root *plaudere*, which means "to clap"; thus an explosion can be imagined as the clapping of the hands of God.

In our anthem, war and the heavens coincide through the flag, a convergence that hinges on the word "star." Shooting star. The four-star general, the pop star, and star-crossed lovers know that stars are much more than distant suns. They can signal praise or fame or destiny; they can stand for the Red Army Faction, Starbucks, Macy's, Converse, Walmart, Satanism (as a pentagram), and the Dallas Stars hockey team. Our fifty states transform into stellar abstractions on the flag's face. The nation is full of starry-eyed dreamers who've taken a shine to all that glints and glitters and detonates but for the blindfold of broad stripes. In *Dialectic of Enlightenment*, Theodor Adorno and Max Horkheimer wrote in 1944 that "the Enlightenment has eradicated the last remnant of its own self-awareness." The stripes, ever broadening, block the light.

Francis Scott Key had a problem with darkness. He was a pro-slavery activist who argued that the taste of the abolitionist "is to associate and amalgamate with the negro," a thought he could not bear since an amalgamation of black and white would inevitably darken the latter. This distaste for darkness—residual, but there nonetheless—casts a shadow on our light-seeking anthem.

The tropes of lightness and darkness—a remnant of our

primordial apprehensions—still function. Light is goodness, knowledge, and love; dark is evil, ignorance, and hate. What if humans, like the implausible creatures in the Mariana Trench, had been bioluminescent from the beginning? What if we could emit light from our own bodies when we needed it? Today, prostheses like flashlights or night-vision goggles or the glow from phone screens guide us in the night, but what if our bodies could make just the right amount of light to maneuver in the dark? I wonder how human bioluminescence would have changed our poems, our holy books, and our anthems. Without the threat of darkness and without a stark contrast between visibility and obscurity, light would have lost most of its figurative shine. The small, green, glowing, genderless beings who hang out in Roswell and Marfa are just humans from the future, with big brains and luminescent bodies, saying hi to their dull-skinned ancestors who haven't yet figured out time travel. Their poems use other metaphors to make knowledge and ignorance lyrical.

There is proof that we want to rush our skin to glow. In his book *Dawn over Zero: The Story of the Atomic Bomb*, William L. Laurence gives his account of the bombing of Nagasaki on August 9, 1945, describing the moment of impact on the ground as viewed from above:

Captain Bock swung around to get out of range; but even though we were turning away in the opposite direction, and despite the fact that it was broad daylight in our cabin, all of us became aware of a giant flash that broke through the dark barrier of our arc welders' lenses and flooded our cabin with an intense light. After the first flash, we removed our glasses, but the light lingered on, a bluish-green light that illuminated the entire sky all around. [. . .] Observers in the tail of our ship saw a giant ball of fire rise as though from the bowels of the earth, belching forth enormous white smoke rings. Next they saw a giant pillar of purple fire, 10,000 feet high, shooting skyward with enormous speed. By the time our ship had made another turn in the direction of the atomic explosion the pillar of purple fire had reached the level of our altitude. Only about forty-five seconds had passed. Awe-struck, we watched it shoot upward like a meteor coming from the earth instead of from outer space, becoming ever more alive as it climbed skyward through the white clouds. It was no longer smoke, or dust, or even a cloud of fire. It was a living thing, a new species of being, born right before our incredulous eyes.

Our anthem is bright, but America wanted to deliver a more radiant message to Japan, one we'd learned in our hymnals: "This little light of mine, I'm gonna let it shine." An utter silence fell after the bombs did, disturbed later by the staticky clicks of curious but vigilant Geiger counters that studied the new flatnesses. In no uncertain terms, we'd beaten out their daylights. How can one explain without science or poetry the new glow that settled in the land's creases and in the smoldering creases of skin? Resplendent epidermal topographies.

Lesson number one: brief, explosive bursts, repeated at regular intervals, are the best way to illuminate a flag. Lesson number two: the best way to defeat war nostalgia is to keep having wars. Most nations have incorporated these lessons into the fabric of their flags. As we reminisced about the '90s, a friend asked me, "Remember the green glow of SCUD missiles over silhouetted minarets?" We have only glowing memories of war: mushroom clouds applauded with glee by crowds wearing sunglasses; Afghan fireworks; shots popped at night across hillscapes, cityscapes, oceanscapes, prairiescapes, across town plazas through the ages; flashes in the underbrush, then naked flashes after Agent Orange; the imagined luster of stockpiled WMDs or of very real IEDs. I wonder, what does the blink of a drone look like? Just as home lighting has undergone a recent transition from incandescent to LED, the war lights will change hue and increase in efficiency. Maybe there will be a much more dangerous laser zeppelin in our combat future, not an acid-trip spectacle but an actual blimplike mother ship equipped with razor-sharp light beams. (I'd forgotten that "laser" is an acronym for "light amplification by stimulated emission of radiation.") Nuclear drones. Body-melting beams. Photon, proton, electron, quantum, quark blitz. Incendiary projectiles launched from an iPhone. The future's so bright, you've got to wear shades. We have good ones—Ray-Ban Aviators—perfected in the 1930s for military pilots. The Enlightenment will just keep getting brighter.

During my '80s childhood, I had a Hasbro toy called a Lite-Brite. It was a triangular light box you plugged in with a plastic screen full of little holes on one side. The kit came with sheets of black construction paper that had color codes printed in white in the shape of a clown's face or a butterfly. After mounting one of these black sheets on the honeycombed screen, you would find the corresponding translucent colored pegs to match up with the codes, punching them through the paper into the hole. Peg by peg, the light from inside the box would reveal its polychromatic brilliance. After filling the black paper with all the right pegs, you'd end up with a dazzling image that looked especially beautiful in the dark. There was something immensely satisfying about punching your way through the pulpy blackness with these little bright pegs. The sound was especially fulfilling, like tiny tears in the firmament. You could see the progress of your enlightenment mission. You were a maker of light. For the more creative souls, there were even blank sheets for your own designs. I was usually disappointed by my own creations, except when I decided to fill every single hole in the screen to make a lawless phantasmagoria. This was the postmodern version of the magic lantern that enchanted people throughout the nineteenth century. With the Lite-Brite, a generation of kids worked quietly away, dialing up the light peg by peg, wired to the outlet in a corner, in solitude. Self-bedazzlement. *Fiat lux.*

Here is an excerpt from Walt Whitman's *Specimen Days* called "The White House by Moonlight," dated February 24, 1863, toward the midpoint of the Civil War:

A spell of fine soft weather. I wander about a good deal, sometimes at night under the moon. Tonight took a long look at the President's house. The white portico—the palace-like, tall, round columns, spotless as snow—the walls also—the tender and soft moonlight, flooding the pale marble, and making peculiar faint languishing shades, not shadows—everywhere a soft transparent hazy, thin, blue moon-lace, hanging in the air—the brilliant and extra-plentiful clusters of gas, on and around the façade, columns, portico, &c.—everything so white, so marbly pure and dazzling, yet soft—the White House of future poems, and of dreams and dramas, there in the soft and copious moon—the gorgeous front, in the trees, under the lustrous flooding moon, full of reality, full of illusion—the forms of the trees, leafless, silent, in trunk and myriad-angles of branches, under the stars and sky—the White House of the land, and of beauty and night—sentries at the gates, and by the portico, silent, pacing there in blue overcoats—stopping you not at all, but eyeing you with sharp eyes, whichever way you move.

Poetry in prose gets no better than this. The White House is a second moon. In the half-light reflected off its surface—a second-order reflection, the sunlight having already reflected off the moon—the adjectives run away with Whitman. They get confused in the half dark, morphing into their opposites. The "peculiar faint languishing shades, not shadows" and "brilliant and extra-plentiful clusters of gas" signal the presence of ghosts at the executive residence. These shades and gases are the umbral and penumbral spirits of the underworld, subtle poltergeist guests loitering at the lawn's edges. The poem's hues are blue and white, red being of too high a frequency for its low-frequency tenor. Even before the arrival of film, Whitman understood the White House as a screen upon which ideas are projected. This architectural symbol would become the nation's movie house, the white cinema upon and inside which every political drama unfolds. Screens divert (distract and entertain); they are made for protection and projection. Whitman dreams of movies as blue as the coats of Union soldiers. The passerby eyes the white spectacle and gets eyed back by blue boys in the dark.

Recently, I had a conversation in a New Haven coffee shop with a young libertarian doctor. Nearly every white, under-age-forty, American man I've met outside the university in the last five years is a libertarian. Go figure. I was reading a book about the cellular consciousness of plants. He was reading *Atlas Shrugged*. Sometimes people with opposing worldviews can have nice conversations. At some point in our discussion, I said, "The Enlightenment is ultimately unsatisfying," a sentence that delighted him even though he disagreed. He still believes that reason can solve every problem. When I'd studied the French Enlightenment with a Diderot specialist back in the day—right after Y2K, when people had lost their minds for no reason—I thought I'd finally found a philosophy that was compatible with my own. The engravings from the *Encyclopédie* reminded me of the kinds of things I wanted to draw: the architectural components of buildings, bodies imagined as machines, the details of plant life, in short, the material phenomena that make up daily experience. I loved the sharpness of the philosophers' brains, tongues, and wit. I imagined a revived salon culture in coffee shops like Kharma Café and Brick Haus in Denton, Texas, where I went to school. At the time, I couldn't read enough Diderot and Voltaire. I found so much eighteenth-century stuff thrilling: I thought *libertinage* was awesome, I read lots of Sade, I celebrated anticlerical radicalism and the horizontalization of hierarchical power structures. But like any total-izing thought system, the Enlightenment had its dark spots. It was full of hypocrisies, shortcomings, and other kinds of murk. This has led some people to say things like, "The Ho-locaust wouldn't have happened without the Enlightenment," which is hypothetical to such a degree that one can't even respond to it (like the other famous hypothetical scenario: "The Holocaust wouldn't have happened if Hitler had gotten into art school"). Instead, I'll stick with my gut feeling about the whole thing: the Enlightenment is ultimately *unsatisfying*.

What does it fail to deliver? Reason is great and all, a decent way to begin solving problems, but rationalism often makes people do sicko things. And somehow, Truth gets a rubbery consistency in the hands of even the most rational thinker. I always thought a dash of common sense could be a corrective for this flaccid stretchability, but no one (includ-ing me) knows what common sense actually is. What then? Faith? Too divisive. Intuition? Too slippery. Emotion? Too volatile. Accumulation of experience? Too varied from person to person. A return to animal instinct? Too bloody. A cus-tomized approach? Too American. So what are we supposed to do? I guess we are forced to operate provisionally (yet an-other word bound to sight, if only in its etymology).

Because the republics of France and the United States. began around the same time, and because they both had many of their shared irons in the Enlightenment fire, I want to put France's national anthem in conversation with America's. An-thems are interesting places to look for clues about a culture's subconscious. "La Marseillaise," composed a couple of decades before "The Star-Spangled Banner," is remarkably grotesque, complete with spilled blood and throat slitting:

Allons enfants de la Patrie,	*Arise, children of the Fatherland,*
Le jour de gloire est arrivé!	*The day of glory has arrived!*
Contre nous de la tyrannie,	*Against us tyranny's*
L'étendard sanglant est levé.	*Bloody flag is raised.*
Entendez-vous dans les campagnes	*Do you hear, in the countryside,*
Mugir ces féroces soldats?	*The roar of those fierce soldiers?*
Ils viennent jusque dans vos bras	*They're coming right into your arms*
Égorger vos fils, vos compagnes!	*To slit the throats of your sons and women!*
Aux armes, citoyens,	*To arms, citizens,*
Formez vos bataillons,	*Form your battalions,*
Marchons, marchons!	*Let's march, let's march!*
Qu'un sang impur	*May impure blood*
Abreuve nos sillons!	*Water our furrows!*

If you've never read the lyrics to "La Marseillaise" before, you may be surprised by their departure from the Frenchman-as-pansy cliché that Americans like to tell themselves. Brutality is just as much a part of French history as it is of American history. Like its American counterpart, "La Marseillaise" is a vertical poem. Perhaps this is a feature of most anthems: verticality. A call to arms is a picking up of weapons, a summoning up of energies. Raised flag, hovering Father, a glorious and upward future. The Father is omnipresent in the French anthem. In fact, its primary theme is filiation and bloodlines. (A Freudian might read the thing as an extended castration fear narrative; during the subsequent guillotine fest called the Terror, France more or less neutered itself.) An interesting thought experiment might be to imagine a more structurally uterine anthem, all about absorbing or incorporating the enemy into the self rather than poking at it. A notable difference between the American and French anthems: people are virtually absent from "The Star-Spangled Banner," except in the references to "we" who watch the skyborne spectacle, while "La Marseillaise" abounds with them. It is an anthropocentric anthem. And implicitly, if the French are human, the enemies (the Prussians and Austrians, when it was composed) are subhuman. For example, the verb *mugir*, translated insufficiently as "roar," can also mean the sound a cow makes. (The English translation, "Do you hear, in the countryside, the moo of those fierce soldiers?" would have decreased some of the anthem's efficiency.) For the French ear, the verb *mugir* calls to mind the bellowing of cattle, but also the roaring of waves or wind; in other words, nonhuman sounds. It is worth noting that the word "barbarian" comes from a root that means stammering or stuttering, the perceived sound of foreigners speaking one's own tongue. This is what animals and foreigners have in common: they're no good at expressing themselves in the vocabulary and grammar that's been declared as righteous. In the anthem, the remote, barbarian roar strikes fear in the hearts of citizens; a specter hovers in the distance and will arrive in time to murder everything you love. The "impure blood" verse suggests that the French are genetically superior to their barbarian enemies, prefiguring the National Socialists' obsession with eugenics. The enemy blood will be put to good use: it will irrigate the fields. (I've always wondered: wouldn't this contaminate the beloved *terroir*?) While in the American anthem, most of the action takes place in the sky, in the French one, everything is earthbound. They've made a blood pact with the land. *Blut und Boden*, yet another Nazi connection. The countryside and the fields' furrows are the deathscape where battles are won and lost. During the trench warfare of World War One, death burrowed its way into the earth like an untamable shrew. Soldiers made their own burials easier by dying halfway underground.

As a fan of small subversions, I always appreciated the reggae rendering of "La Marseillaise" called "Aux armes *et cætera*" (1979) by Serge Gainsbourg, one of my favorite provocateurs. He recorded the song in and under the influence of Kingston, Jamaica, inviting Rita Marley, Bob Marley's widow, to sing backup. The chorus of the song says, "To arms, *et cætera*" instead of "To arms, citizens," because, as Gainsbourg claims, the song's composer Rouget de Lisle had written "*et cætera*" instead of the full repeated chorus on the original handwritten document. Rather than mocking the anthem, as many accused him of doing, he was faithfully reproducing the song's original lyrics. In a video version, Serge is shown alternately in front of one of the Arc de Triomphe sculptures known as *La Marseillaise* and in some dark interior listening to himself on an album, all the while smoking either a cigarette or a fat spliff. Toward the end of the clip, he watches with his usual phlegmatic gaze and disheveled presence as a military memorial ceremony takes place before him. Gazing on with anthropological detachment, he lights a new smoke just after a shot of the eternal flame at the foot of the monument. Gainsbourg, the man who burned a five-hundred-franc note on live television, is clearly unmoved by national sentiment and symbol. (He was always rather a pan-national figure whose music disregarded administrative borders.) There is a lot of smoke in Gainsbourg's video but very little fire. I read this as his depiction of France as a nation whose flame, growing ever smaller, continues to produce lots and lots of blinding smoke. The low flame of the Enlightenment fills the sky with billows, like an Icelandic volcano.

I wonder what it feels like to be French and to sing "La Marseillaise" aloud today, especially given the racial tensions, the anti-Semitism, the anti-Arab angst, and other forms of xenophobia that characterize contemporary France. My students generally find these lyrics appalling in their violence. In terms of literal bloodletting, "The Star-Spangled Banner" is more innocuous than the French anthem. Its verses are bloodless. But the French would counter, probably rightly, that America, uncomfortable looking directly in the face of problems, tends to gloss over things. Everything is like the sun to us: don't stare into it lest ye be blinded. America isn't less prone to violence and racism; *au contraire*, we just like to hide these things behind political correctness and happy faces, Band-Aids on a gangrene wound. The French find political correctness ridiculous because it simply forces people to take their opinions underground, but this judgment stems from a partial misconception of the term. Despite its name, this kind of expression does not simply involve self-censorship with the aim of getting elected. Political correctness means thinking about what you say before you say it, and this is a skill of great value, one that is still sorely lacking in the public space and especially online. Political correctness asks you to imagine what it would be like to be on the receiving end of your comments. It asks for a little equanimity in speech, some brainpower behind your words.

The origin of America as a republic involved an insurrection against Britain, far away, across the pond. The origin of France as a republic involved an insurrection against itself. And this makes a huge difference, whether you aim your bullets outward or inward. In this respect, the Civil War is more comparable to the French Revolution. In a journal entry from April 16, 1865, the day after Abraham Lincoln's assassination, Walt Whitman wrote that Lincoln "was assassinated—but the Union was not assassinated—*ça ira*!" This last expression, which means roughly "It will continue" or "It will be all right" in French, was the title of one of the most popular songs during the French Revolution. One of its verses goes: *Ah! ça ira, ça ira, ça ira!/ Les aristocrates on les pendra! / Et quand on les aura tous pendus / On leur fichera la pelle au cul* ("We'll hang the aristocrats! / And when we've hanged them all / We'll stick a shovel up their ass"). Whitman's application of this French phrase to Civil War–torn America is no accident; both conflicts were the result of domestic clefts. The nation, he believed, would not be bisected again, even through extreme acts meant to sow discord, like John Wilkes Booth's assassination of Lincoln. Another difference between the French and American revolutions: America has no residual aristocracy. The power of even the Kennedys, the pop stars, the gazillionaires, or whomever one imagines as the equivalent of an aristocracy in the States is nothing compared with the absolute power involved in monarchy and the castelike hierarchy of the ancien régime. I can't articulate exactly how, but, as an outsider, one has the constant impression in France that the pecking order is still very much in place. The Sun King's spirit was never fully extinguished. The American mythology of the self-made person diverges wildly from the French mythology of inherited eminence or lowliness. Our culture is half Protestant work ethic, half lottery ticket: we believe firmly in the virtues and potentialities of both. One's willingness to work hard every day usually does not preclude the occasional purchase of a Mega Millions Quick Pick. Before our current oligarchic gravitation, the belief seemed to hold that anyone could luck out or work up to some position of importance. People seem less inclined to believe this at the moment, for good reason. While there are still enough success stories to suggest that triumph is available to everyone, we recognize how dim the odds have become for the majority.

So the origins of both the French and the American republics are lit by Enlightenment values, such as the reliance on reason and the belief in the power of the individual. But because the light source was Europe, things were more dim in America. Although we had many of the same grievances against the European monarchy as the French, we had no domestic aristocracy to dethrone. We were youngsters away from our parents, longing for a light of our own. Through the centuries, we've lit many of our own fires, burning a few barns and witches and crosses and books and bridges and flags. In our pyromaniac hands, almost everything is combustible. Once we got our own little light shining, we made it our logo of a Manifest Destiny. We wanted to be the world's beacon. The light of genius has always been particularly dear to us: Edison's lightbulb, the most famous though not the first, was figuratively and literally incandescent, proof of a bright mind; Yale's motto is *lux et veritas,* light and truth; and think of the Silicon Valley illuminati (Sun Microsystems is a bright name). Have a look at the way light works in the painting from the nineteenth century called *The Genius of America* by the French artist Adolphe Yvon. This classically influenced, large-scale allegory is one way to depict brilliance, clearly the vision of an Old European. The picture is half flooded with white light. But American genius is more auroral in nature, twisting and turning in the sky like a living rainbow. In America, the rainbow is not just a play of prismal light; it is a symbol of inclusion and the unstoppability of love. It is LeVar Burton showing us a book on *Reading Rainbow.* The rainbow's name is Roy G. Biv and he serves as a symbol of Christianity, imported Irish mysticism, the Cheer Bear from *The Carebears*, Rainbow Brite, Lucky Charms cereal, Pride parades, NBC, old Apple, or United Way. The universe gives us the gift of a double rainbow. Oh my God, what does it *mean*?

France gave us a gift once, too: Lady Liberty, with her torch held high. She crossed the Atlantic—known to millions as the Middle Passage—in little boxes to be erected as a human beacon, her head itself a sun emitting figurative rays of light. She faces out to sea, like the figurehead of a ship, the SS *U.S.A.* Her real name is *La Liberté éclairant le monde* ("Liberty Enlightening the World"), symbolically binding France and the United States in their shared Enlightenment project. I agree with Viktor Frankl, who recommended that "the Statue of Liberty be supplemented by a Statue of Responsibility on the West Coast." Together, these two sisters could rein in the thick-skulled pseudofreedoms that inevitably backfire: "I assert my freedom to say dumb and untrue things very loudly with zero thought toward the consequences of words!" "I assert my freedom to hunt with an AK-47 and show my nine-year-old how to love violence! And I don't owe you anything if he goes on a rampage at sixteen!" Because 'Murica. While Immanuel Kant argued that "Enlightenment is man's emergence from his self-imposed immaturity," we might agree that there is a pinnacle to maturation that, once reached, subsequently risks becoming a steep-pitched downward slope. The progressive infantilization of the States is clear, and France has many of its own examples of a juvenile tendency in its culture. Lady Liberty is now Teen Liberty and the stately stone tablet she clutches in her hand, which used to read JULY IV MDCCLXXVI (1776), has morphed into a digital tablet that reads OMG LMFAO.

In 1994, Soundgarden released a song called "Black Hole Sun." I didn't see the video at the time because my parents had canceled cable already back in the '80s, partly due to the excessive sex and violence, and partly because my mom once walked in to find six-year-old me and my three-year-old brother watching MTV and jumping on the couch, singing Twisted Sister's "We're Not Gonna Take It" at the top of our lungs. I recently watched the Soundgarden video and found in it all the tropes of millennial fear and celestial trembling so characteristic of the late twentieth century. In what seems to be a picture-perfect American neighborhood where people barbecue and sunbathe underneath a hyperbolically blue sky, a sign carried by a group of believers announces, "The End Is

Nigh." As this end draws closer, people's faces contort wildly, eyes bulging and smiles stretching their faces like rubber bands. When it finally arrives, the doomsday sun becomes a dark vacuum that sucks up the neighborhood and the whole earth. White picket fences are swallowed up by a black hole sun. Dark matter trumps light. This emblem of Gen-X nihilism—a clear critique of bourgeois narratives of the good life—reveals the '90s as a strange decade in the timeless battle between darkness and light. The subterranean cultures of Goth, black metal, and satanism flourished; mainstream TV thought a lot about the dark underbelly of civilization (*Twin Peaks, X-Files, Cops, Buffy the Vampire Slayer, Unsolved Mysteries*). This continues today, particularly in fictional crime series, which astound in their brutality. I'm always at a loss for words when I see how gross and desperate for ratings these shows have become. I'm no lily-livered viewer; I like my share of disturbing thoughts played out on film. But what is so unsettling about the crime shows is the unprecedented amount of bad faith they display. They're perpetually involved in a moralizing tug-of-war that shows in great detail all of the horrendous acts you should not engage in: pedophilia, incest, spousal abuse, prostitution, exploitive porn making, torture, stalking, voyeurism, exhibitionism, cheating, homicide, suicide, infanticide, mass shootings, sexual harassment, kidnapping, sex slavery, you name it. There is hardly a taboo subject that hasn't been broached. The bad faith part of all this is that the producers pretend not to condone the stuff. But the negligible gestures they make in order to show disapproval are pathetic and glaring. We see similar bad faith on network news. I recall a report about a little girl, maybe around nine years old, whose parents had created a Web site with photos of her in all sorts of provocative poses and skimpy clothing. For a fee, her "fans" could mail her clothes in which she would be photographed, and the pictures would be posted on her site. Clearly, this is exploitive stuff on the part of the parents. But the sicker part is how the network—I don't remember which one but they all more or less do the same thing—reported this transformation of a nine-year-old kid into a masturbatory object. The report showed the suggestive pictures as the journalist spoke in a reproachful tone. At least be honest about the exploitation. Don't pretend that you're reporting on this kid for any reason other than to cash in on Lolita. Networks know that the nymphet, Humbert Humbert's loin flame and the national daughter of France and America, makes everybody's cup brim with tiddles. This is the kind of darkness against which many Gen-Xers tried to mobilize their energies. The perceived squeaky cleanness of '80s family life, business, and politics was revealed as a thin veneer over thick masses of malevolence. They knew about the shadowy hearth at home. And they suspected gloom in the offices of CEOs, congressmen, and clergy.

In 2010, the Texas musician and hell-raiser Ray Wiley Hubbard released an album and a song of the same title: "A. Enlightenment B. Endarkenment (Hint: There Is No C)." This is the phrase whispered over and over to the song's narrator by a black sparrow, and then, "Heaven pours down rain and lightning bolts." Do these lightning bolts bring enlightenment or endarkenment? Do we have a choice? Hubbard was clearly thinking of the end when composing the album; among its other songs are "Every Day Is the Day of the Dead" and "The Four Horsemen of the Apocalypse." I wonder if it is mainly old folks who proclaim most fervently the end of days (Hubbard released the album in his sixties); maybe they want to generalize their own impending end, unable to imagine a universe that will continue without them. The album cover shows Hubbard's headless body, a sword in one hand and his own decapitated head in the other, wearing his usual tinted glasses. The image implies that he beheaded himself, like a nobleman of the ancien régime pulling the guillotine rope with his own aristocratic crown lodged in the apparatus. Does Headless Hubbard, eyes shielded from the brightness of apocalyptic lightning bolts or of the Enlightenment, suggest that we are decapitating ourselves? Is our Endarkenment self-induced? Will the four horsemen of the apocalypse be headless horsemen, unable to see in which direction they're riding? There is a lot of suspicion toward the Enlightenment in our times and a new nihilism that wants to precipitate total darkness. If light is truth, our choreographed illumination resembles that of Studio 54 or *Soul Train*: unexpected colors and intensities pulse and vault before our eyes in a reserve of darkness. What is Enlightenment? We ask the question again and again and decide on and off that it is good, constantly changing the potency and dosage of light we prefer. At this particular moment, America seems at a loss on what to do with Enlightenment values like rationality, freethinking, *libertinage*, and skepticism. Very sane and very insane people make identical arguments about them, and people in between stay mercurial on the subject. Is the choice between Enlightenment and Endarkenment a false choice? How can we make sense of the horrible and the beautiful things we've done as a nation? To what extent can we take credit or responsibility for this darkness and light?

Civilizations are often depicted as people, with a birth, maturity, decline, and death. Who knows what form America's end will take or what our final words will be. It is said that on his deathbed, Goethe's last words were, "Mehr Licht!" (More light!) Perhaps ours will be the same.

The Great American Irony Binge

Remember [. . .] that women, children, and revolution-
ists hate irony, which is the negation of all saving instincts, of
all faith, of all devotion, of all action.

—JOSEPH CONRAD, *Under Western Eyes*

America is on its tiptoes, peeking around corners and through the slit in the blinds, skirting this uncomfortable encounter or that one. We have recourse to the diversion, the decoy, the sprint, or feigned ignorance. These refined, evasive techniques make it easier to elude those who might corner us with hard questions about what we really mean. Ours is a shifty population, apprehensive of the upfront. Everything is in disguise, masquerading as something other than itself.

From the '90s onward, a specific kind of rhetoric has draped itself over American culture: irony, that beloved tool with the power to humble one's opponents, to help discern between people who get it and those who don't, to fight back when one is in the minority, to make life's traumas and tribulations a little easier to handle. Some of the best writers in history share a finely tuned ironic sensibility: Diderot, Musil, Woolf, Malaparte, Svevo; they understood how to properly massage that discrepancy between what is said and what is meant. Our great satirists used it to tangle up their enemies; down became up, up became down, with gravity undone in their pages. Written in the eighteenth century, Swift's "A Modest Proposal" still delights. His text had teeth. With a careful assemblage of fake pragmatism and sympathy, Swift was able to stage his reader's shock to arrive at a very specific moment, this sentence: "A young healthy child well nursed, is, at a year old, a most delicious nourishing and wholesome food, whether stewed, roasted, baked, or boiled; and I make no doubt that it will equally serve in a fricassee, or a ragout." I wonder how many jaws fell when they reached that line. Swift used irony—very conspicuously—to comment on his moment. When administered in the right doses and in the right context, irony is just about the most civically powerful mechanism available to the average person.

But what was powerful about irony was its status as exception: it was mastered by the quick-witted and deployed with discernment, not as an everyday, go-to response but as an anomaly with impact. The right word at the right time and place could come off like a bottle rocket. Something strange has happened to this venerated rhetorical device. The public space has become a kind of swampscape: irony, irony as far as the eye can see, stretching out before us like the bog in which Aqualung warms his feet. To make a gluttonous comparison, we've stuffed ourselves with irony the way we've stuffed ourselves with vaguely edible things slick with high-fructose drippage. In a dig at Emerson's too-concentrated, too-perfect pages, Walt Whitman wrote: "How good [. . .] is good butter, good sugar. But to be eating nothing but sugar and butter all the time!"

That dynamic duo Stewart and Colbert come to mind as prime examples of public figures who've found a way to merge comedy and politics in their performances, using irony in a politically serviceable way. They back up their ironic maneuvers with substance. Comedy news is a perfectly reasonable place to find irony. My beef has nothing to do with these guys, who are simply doing what comedians have always done. What is agitating is the leakage of irony into everyday life: our clothes, politics, gestures, the evening news, and everywhere on the Web.

I have some ideas about why and how this happened, but first, I'd like to sort through the various meanings of irony to get to the one that has been buzzing around our heads of late. What does irony even mean? Tomes and tomes of scholarship have been produced on the subject, I think mostly by Germans. The word seems to have two ordinary uses. The first, à la Alanis Morissette, refers to a situation in which something happens contrary to the way it is expected to: "It's ironic that he was hit by a car the day he won the lottery." When I write of the contemporary irony binge, I mean the second kind of irony, which involves an intentional incongruity between what is said and what is meant. The word's early Greek root *eironeia* means dissimulation, which shows that irony was conceived as a cloaking device. Sarcasm, a more specific, negatively connoted use of irony, has an etymology that points toward carnal violence: the Greek *sarkazein*, from which the word "sarcasm" derives, means to strip off the flesh. If sarcasm is a frontal attack, irony is a false flag.

Picture a T-shirt with the phrase I'M WEARING THIS T-SHIRT IRONICALLY printed across the chest. We have veered outside the boundaries of rhetoric. How can someone wear a T-shirt ironically? What is the opposite of this? Wearing the T-shirt sincerely? Authentically? Or even just neutrally? That one can wear something ironically seems at first either absurd or inconceivable. But it is possible, isn't it? Anything can be worn ironically. A comparison: the way Magnum P.I. wore his mustache has nothing to do with the way a hipster—more or less extinct by the time these words reach you—wears his. Magnum, framed by the '80s, was consciously doing what he could to make his sex appeal surge. He believed in the erotic potential of that lip hair. Most everyone did. America tacitly agreed that the mustache could make a man out of someone, that it held occult powers of arousal.

Fashion is a kind of collective complicity, a shared commitment to an aesthetic gambit. There were surely people in the 1970s and 1980s who found the mustache to be ridiculous. But testimony and material vestiges of the time show that for the mainstream, the 'stache was a legitimate strategy of attraction. And what of the hipster's mustache? Isn't he aiming for sexiness in his own way? Doesn't he ultimately wish to attract rather than repulse? Of course he does. But in his case, the mustache is citational. He is quoting the fur-lipped hunks from the days of yore, their sylvan chests forested with hair, their shorts the size of ziplock sandwich bags. Since then, those hunks, even the most Adonis-like among them, have mutated into ludicrous caricatures. The hipster knows a mustache without an explanatory footnote is probably foolish to someone he might attempt to attract, so he builds a little preemptive, citational goofiness into his look to avoid the possibility that someone might think he *actually* wants to look like Magnum P.I. "Because that would be ridiculous," he says to himself. The layer of irony allows him to toy with the look as a possible tool of attraction without committing wholeheartedly to it. At the first sign of criticism or repugnance from anyone inside his current or potential social circle, he can show his aesthetic superiority by pointing out his critic's mistake: having taken him seriously. He admits in advance that he is masked so he can spare himself that humbling moment: "And I would have gotten away with it, too, if it wasn't for you meddling kids!" From ugly-sweater parties to purposely silly-voiced indie bands, from TV news that prioritizes often ironic entertainment over information to middle-class students ironically hanging out at the local dive bar among blue-collar workers, irony is the white noise of our time.

Because this phenomenon has arrived in America at a relatively clearly defined moment—from the 1990s to the present—it could be described as a generational problem. So if the ironic reflex is indeed a generational issue, it might be helpful to think through what the word "generation" even means. This word is slick as an eel, slipping through the fingers of social scientists and everyone else. When it comes to describing the relationships between people and the moment in which they live, there is a shortage of words in everyday language. In English, the word "generation" can mean the division that separates me and the people born around the same time as me from my mother and people her age, and then from my grandmother and people her age. Sometimes the word "cohort" is used to describe this social, natally bound unit. "Generation" can also mean all of the people who are alive at any given moment. This use of the term would group me, my mother, and my grandmother into one unit, since we are all simultaneously accessing the same world. The three of us watched TV as the *Challenger* shuttle exploded. We read about Rwanda as it happened. We all remember what we were doing when 9/11 occurred. We witnessed together the election of the first black president of the United States. These shared experiences create a kind of generational intimacy even if we are of different ages. Another difficulty in forging a vocabulary of generations is the messiness and noncorrespondence of generational breaks, stemming from the fact that some people have kids very early, some very late, and the neatness of periodization rarely works anyway. For example, my own cousins are a mixture of Millennials and Gen-Xers (like myself), but I know a Millennial whose cousin happens to be a Boomer. Furthermore, I've met Gen-Xers who behave a lot like Boomers, and other Gen-Xers who have all of the signature characteristics of Millennials, so "Gen-Xer" is hardly a stable category. Geography complicates matters more; within the vast geological spill that is the United States, some cultural phenomena take off more quickly in some regions, more slowly in others. Not to mention the way race, class, and other factors complicate the question. So people of the same cohort may have completely different experiences when faced with the culture of their moment.

I'm certain someone has already created a sophisticated vocabulary for talking about these relationships, but these words have yet to enter the realm of everyday speech. For the sake of convenience, let's call all of us who are alive in the now a "generation" (this includes me, my mother, and my grandmother) and let's call each age group (Boomers, Gen-Xers, Millennials) a "cohort." So is the ironic reflex a generation problem or a cohort problem? I would say some of both, but the cohort has been more affected, particularly younger Gen-Xers and all Millennials. Even within this age demographic, I would guess that one could find the most evidence of ironic living among middle-class, educated, white people in urban and suburban areas and in college towns. However, because this is the class that often has the most input in the mediatized world (TV, advertising, Internet, print publications), its irony becomes an omnipresent haze that hovers wherever the human meets media. That is to say: everywhere.

The mother tongue of basically everyone born in the U.S. from the mid-1960s to the present is "Ironese." Our fluency makes us comprehensible to one another but incomprehensible to everyone else. So, despite an inner craving for sincerity or forthrightness, we have no language in which to express this desire. The good news is: foreign languages can be learned.

If the preferred rhetorical figure of Gen-X was litotes, for Gen-Y it is hyperbole. And the most hyperbolic representative of a certain kind of aesthetic excess is the hipster. The hipster movement has more or less expired, having exhausted itself through the mainstream, but it is one of the most revelatory phenomena of first-world life. Rarely admitting its own existence, since few wear the hipster label proudly, this strange elitism operates moodily and relies upon the virtual for most of its energy. The hipster is a kind of self-aware jester or, better yet, a harlequin. Harlequin, or Arlecchino in Italian, is a stock character from the sixteenth-century commedia dell'arte theater tradition who is quick, light, resplendent, and survives with his street smarts. He dresses in gaudy, loud colors, is slender and acrobatic, and is always in need of money. He is clownish, anarchic in behavior, and dependent on the flashes of wit that get him out of tight situations. He somersaults recklessly from adventure to adventure. Always slipping through the fingers, he can never quite be caught. As a specialist of the cosmetic, he represents all that is surface. Today's deep ironist is a modernized Harlequin. The latest model of this figure, the hipster, has access to a whole world of underground culture you've never heard of. He strives to be an entire avant-garde movement packaged in a single body. Pop culturally, he is always one step ahead of you. As a *beau parleur*, or smooth talker, he finds ways to round off the rough edges of conversation, conveying a kind of cultural competency that leaves you feeling in a perpetual state of lack. He scoffs at your paltry knowledge of bands and fashionable drugs, changes his tastes once he sees others have begun to catch on, rolls his eyes when you try to understand him. He abhors naïveté. By making himself preemptively into a joke, he has shielded himself from all potential critiques.

Like the hippie in the 1960s, the hipster is the human

crystallization of a distinct cultural juncture. No other figure better captures the specificity of the now. In all his or her silliness, the hipster conveys an absolute lack of faith in systems. No longer does this group—composed largely of middle- to upper-middle-class, white, educated people—believe in the fixity of categories or in authoritative voices. Everything has failed too many times. Because they have nothing to which they can pin their convictions, they instead make a mockery of everything. No one is exempt from this ridicule: not corporations, institutions of state and church, or even themselves. Few could blame them for this maneuver, given the perpetual moral bankruptcy of most institutions against which they lodge their implicit critiques. It is tempting to stick one's tongue out at the politicians who sabotage, at the companies that manipulate, at the establishments that lie. This gesture is nothing new. What is maybe new is the lumping together of most aspects of culture into one mockable whole. Civilization has become one big punch line.

At first, turning everything into a circus of the absurd could be read as a noble move, something akin to what the Surrealists and other major constituents of the avant-garde were doing at the beginning of the twentieth century when Duchamp called a urinal "art" and critiqued the arbitrariness of institutionalized taste. But what exactly is the message of the hipster? What is the hipster resisting? Tradition? No, the hipster celebrates old-fashioned living as much as novelty. Conformity? No, there is much too much sameness in the aesthetic for it to be about the celebration of uniqueness. Capitalism? No: as the apex of our cynicism, hipsterism participates actively in capitalism even while deriding it. In fact, our total crypto-bourgeois-ification is embodied in this tableau: the hipster getting his handlebar waxed at the Art of Shaving.

I believe that the hipster class is composed mostly of well-meaning people who are smart, attentive, and informed about many of the world's injustices. But because they cannot reconcile their own relatively lucky circumstances and the suffering of others and because they have no faith in the institutions that claim to want to fix these injustices, they use the defense mechanism of total negation in order to cope. Even if you are twenty-three years old, living under a mountain of student debt, unable to find a job, and aware that yours is the first social cohort in a while that will likely be worse off than the preceding one, you still must admit that your circumstances are preferable to those of many people of your same age across the globe. You can vote, you can eat, you can go see shows. And even if you're tempted to lash out at the forces who've left you with this debt or who've made you jittery when attending large-scale public events for fear of a terrorist attack, you're pretty certain that these are unsolvable problems. What do you do with this helplessness? The family-making frenzy and shopping fever of the Boomers didn't work. The nihilism and slacker posture of the Gen-Xers didn't work. What about a little levity, like that old song Peggy Lee made famous, where she sings, "Is that all there is? If that's all there is, my friend, then let's keep dancing. Let's break out the booze and have a ball." When things are broken and there's no way to fix them, the endless adult-child's party with its intoxicating antilogic and colored lights blinking to the beat pushes the dark night away outside the steamed-up windows.

If the present is unbearable, there are a couple of options

on where to turn for comfort: either to the past (vintage material culture, outmoded hobbies and fashions, photo filters that make the new look old) or the future (All Tomorrow's Parties, digital futures, what's going to happen next season). And to deal with the present when it's in your face, there are countless handy devices and substances to numb and distract beyond worry.

As far as aesthetics go, the hipster finds relief in surrounding herself with kitsch objects. The Czech writer Milan Kundera wrote, "Kitsch is the absolute denial of shit." A possible reading of this declaration is that kitsch refuses the scale of values that labels one thing as superior to another. Hipsterism, through its purposeful cultivation of ugliness, seems to try to dismantle what historical inertia and semiofficial institutions of taste (fashion blogs, advertising agencies, celebrity opinions, etc.) have promoted as ideal, such as the buxom blonde with a tan or the muscleman. The buxom blonde is replaced by the nerd girl with messy hair and quirky ill-fitting clothes, and the muscleman is replaced by the angular-bodied boy wearing a conspicuous mustache and some random accessory in neon orange. One must at least pretend to be comfortable with ugliness. A skit from *Portlandia* beautifully summarizes this problem: a public service announcement, sponsored by the Portland Nerd Council, shows a cute hipster woman in a bar describing herself as a "big nerd," while an authentically nerdy guy named Brian explains awkwardly the difference between someone who is actually a nerd and someone who feigns nerdhood. Brian tells the viewer that he wears his glasses to see, not as fashion accessories. He is too heavy to fit into skinny jeans. He concludes his critique with this statement, "A real nerd is ashamed to be called a nerd. So please. Get real. If you're not a nerd, don't call yourself one." The kind of false posturing that Brian denounces represents fashion's attempt to appropriate ugliness. Hoping to colonize and thus neutralize all that is unappealing, this appropriation of the ugly makes the faux nerd feel as if she belongs to a community of undesirables, that she is a freakishly delicious social exile. Does she really want to share the nerd's destiny? Alas, she is but a nerd tourist. . . . It is implausible that she will ever need to spend an evening alone.

But hipsters do not have a monopoly on irony. This decade has witnessed the slow corporatization of irony as companies have found more and more clever ways to turn marketing campaigns into snide, self-referential instruments of persuasion. Some examples: Take a flight on Virgin America and you will see a safety video with a blah-voiced narrator who is too cool for school. "For the point zero zero zero one percent of you who have never operated a seat belt before, it works like this," he says, in a bored, condescending tone. Like many commercials these days, the safety video pokes fun at its own format with a kind of world-weary savvy, attempting to distinguish itself as more self-aware than its competitors. Regardless, Virgin America is still a hulking corporate entity. Its ironic posture does not change this. Even though the safety video is not technically a commercial, this genre functions as an advertisement, as it perpetuates a particular brand image and the attitude of a company. Virgin grunts really hard, trying to be hip. It is the only airline I know of that plays electronic lounge music at the check-in desk. Its planes glow inside with soft pinkish-purple lighting, a phony simulation of some VIP back room in an upscale nightclub. The safety video participates in this exclusionary effort that makes Virgin out to be the cool kids' airline. Of course the frequent flier (aka jet-setter) has no use for a safety video. As a member of the rhodium-plated, double-diamond, petroleum-platinum class, she boards first and yawns through the video over her pomegranate cocktail.

Another example of the corporatization of irony is the Kotex tampon commercial about the ridiculousness of tampon commercials, in which a woman wryly tells how much she just loves being on her period. The standard tropes of tampon commercials—soft music, women in free-flowing dresses, nature and sunshine—play during her voice-over, while she says things like "I just want to run on a beach" and "I like to twirl, maybe in slow motion, and I do it in my white spandex." Just like the shrewd narrator of the Virgin flight safety video, this narrator tries to convince the target audience that Kotex is done with the tired conventions of advertising, that Kotex understands that the consumer is too smart for such routine tactics, and that this company offers an alternative to such nonsense. Commercials have always used humor to persuade, but the new ironic iterations seem to announce the end of advertising even as they sustain it. A consumer who is actually smart and paying attention will see that the corporations behind these new campaigns are not actually any different from the corporations behind the old campaigns. They've simply gotten more stealthy. Has the verdict that corporations are people caused this new chumminess, with companies buddying up and trying to share our acute sense of humor? They are desperate for us to friend them on Facebook, after all.

The corporatization of irony participates in the larger

imperative today that absolutely everything be entertaining. We don't want the news if it isn't perkily delivered. We want good-looking journalists who are never fazed by the almost consistently bad news they deliver. They segue cheerily from a segment about military rape to a segment on Ricin-laced letters addressed to politicians, adding just enough seriousness to face and voice so as to maintain the illusion that they are more than just pretty people hired to read a script. The phenomenon of pressing information into a delightfully entertaining format has something to do with the loss of the desire to compartmentalize. We want a combination Pizza Hut and Taco Bell. We want our friends to come with benefits. We want our kids to be our buddies. Our most beloved singers are also entrepreneurs and actors. Our phones manage our lives. Every experience should be streamlined into one convenient accretion, a veritable Walmart world. We seek out the coagulation of culture, in which the cells amass themselves into ever-larger, all-consuming units. Let human achievement congeal into one solid mass. Let our cultivation curdle.

Maybe individuals have taken cues from these corporations and begun to work irony into their everyday lives. Or is it the inverse? Was it the people who gave the first cues? Regardless, from the company to the individual, from the public to the private sphere, the dusts of irony have settled on everyday life in the United States. Compare the kinds of talk you overhear in the street with talk from a couple of decades ago (if you were alive then). Compare the decoration in people's homes, what people wear, what people do in their free time, what people watch on TV. Watch twenty minutes of an old Walter Cronkite broadcast, then watch twenty minutes of CNN. Chances are, through this juxtaposition, the levity and weightlessness I've described in these new broadcasting voices become stabbingly obvious. I think I've seen Brian Williams more on comedy shows than I have on the *NBC Nightly News*. Perhaps it's merely a taste question, but I for one would be happy with a news report minus the snide double entendres and bubbleheadedness. As they used to say, "Just the facts, ma'am."

So from indie to mainstream culture, irony has become one of the primary means of expression in our age for a certain social class, a signature of distinction and a marker of who is in the club and who isn't. Not getting it means instant exclusion, and given the socioeconomic lines dividing who abuses irony and who is oblivious to it, it has become the litmus test for determining who belongs solidly to the middle- to upper-middle class.

Self-infantilization is another hallmark of our moment. Do you know any thirty-year-old men in cargo shorts and a silly T-shirt who play video games in their free time? Do you know grown women who dress like they're back in sixth grade, all glittery and pink? Do you hear parents with their children and have a difficult time distinguishing who the adults are in that relationship? Have you seen adults with zero impulse control throwing a fit when something goes wrong? Whether at the airport, the dentist's office, the grocery store, or in the street, this kind of behavior is almost the norm rather than the exception. Perhaps adults seek refuge in their own childhood because the world is getting more dangerous and unstable. But is it actually? Maybe it's just that twenty-four-hour news channels have to fill the hours with something, and everyone knows that happy news doesn't sell. Hate and bombs and controversy are much more entertaining. In his beautiful book *The Sense of an Ending*, Frank Kermode writes about apocalyptic narratives and illustrates how in these depictions, the end must always be near. The nearness of the ending is a good excuse to postpone responsibility and resuscitate those moments nostalgia says were the best in life. Never have people so willingly regressed. Adulthood now equals the right to wear flip-flops to work and play Angry Birds until four in the morning if you want. Feels like freedom.

But here, a strange paradox arises: children enter puberty unprecedentedly quickly these days, probably because of the hormones in food or some other such human-initiated change to the biological fabric of the body. It is more and more common for girls to start their periods at nine years old or even younger. However, while the reproductive ability announces itself early in comparison to our forebears, there is a drag in behavioral maturation. Have you ever seen photos of teenagers in the nineteenth century? They look old already, with a kind of solemnity in the creases around their eyes and their unsmiling faces. Life then was less buffered by media in comparison to today; people were faced starkly with the real. For most, there was a connectedness to the seasons, to the land, and one's labor was bound inextricably to survival in the most elementary way. Leafing through the great album of human faces, one sees people in 1900, 1920, and 1940 who look very little like people today. (Every once in a while on the street, I catch a glimpse of a face from 1910, particularly when traveling in Europe. The fantastical mind might imagine that this person is a vampire.) Even flipping through my mother's high school yearbook from the 1970s, I notice that those girls looked like women and the boys looked like men. Regardless of the hairstyles and clothing, something in their faces exudes grown-ness.

And what of the teenager today? Membership in the teen-age club, which officially includes only ages thirteen through nineteen, can be renewed now without restriction. Today, adolescence can be prolonged until age twenty, age thirty, age forty. (Time will tell how the fortysomething man-boys will behave when they've turned eighty.) We can put our income toward adult versions of the toys we always wanted, protracting those hours of joy truncated by our parents when we were small.

The theory goes that because of longer life expectancies, people are no longer in a rush to get their lives going. There is no need to barrel toward full maturity by age eighteen, taking on the burdens of family and vocation, when you will likely live to be eighty or older. This argument is not totally convincing. At least speaking from my own perspective, I am not at all cognizant of my potential life expectancy, and even if I were, I'm not sure my conviction that I'll live to be one hundred would make me consciously wear a T-shirt with She-Ra on it. If I wear her on my shirt, it works more as a cohort signature I can bear in public to show my affiliation with the 1980s. Like a kind of anticipatory AARP, the conscious sporting of generational identification markers (other than one's own skin) denotes solidarity and cohesion of a cohort that is slipping away from the center of things.

Aging gracefully is refused in favor of the trappings of perpetual youth. Not in that striving-to-be-wrinkle-free kind of way, which has obsessed people for centuries, but in a let-me-keep-my-thumb-in-my-mouth kind of way. And children need parents, of course. If the American populace is willing to regress into childhood, it shouldn't be surprised that there are some interested parties very eager to step in and play the role of the parent. Who are these parents? The usual suspects: State, Media, Corporation. We salute our caretakers through the bars of our crib.

State: Baby-proof our houses. Save us from responsibility. Provide baby monitors at every cribside. Protect us from ourselves.

Media: Dazzle us with your sparkles. We want formulaic news, simplified narratives, facile categories, and pre-chewed news. Feed our self-centeredness.

Corporation: Give us our hypoallergenic, lavender-scented ultrasensitive limited edition Pampers. Let us eat Hostess Cakes. Sell us our problems and the solutions to those problems.

What are the characteristics of childhood we see in many adults today? Narcissism, gluttony, bullying, loudness, excess, lack of self-control, distraction, flightiness, and the incapacity to anticipate consequences, among others. People have always said that the children are our future. Now, we've given a new meaning to the cliché by turning ourselves consciously into babies.

The not-so-distant past gives clues about how we got here. A diligent historian could probably trace the current state of things back to the early days of modernity or even before, but I'll look toward a less distant past—the 1990s—for some clues about how irony and self-infantilization have become the norm. Postmodernism: a word that no one really likes, a word that means too much and too little at the same time. Let's at least agree that in the second half of the twentieth century, categories that had held up with relative stability over time began to deteriorate and that we watched this deterioration with total interest, pens at attention, trying to record the whole thing as it happened. When one is constantly watching oneself, waiting to document the next move for posterity, the one being watched becomes hesitant. Being observed makes one fidgety yet constipative, eager to do something—the right thing—but at a loss as to exactly what that thing might be. It was the moment of theory explosion in academia; everyone was full of ideas about how to describe and explain everything, complete with new hyphenated jargon and various disciplines piggybacking on one another. Perhaps at that time, there was also the general belief that history was full, that there was nothing new to be done, that from then on, innovation would simply mean reordering culture. This reordering, however, did not involve simply citing old songs, movies, and commercials without bias. Often, the citations pointed toward the inherent ridiculousness or naïveté of earlier cultural production, or toward the possibility of corrupting even the most noble of the arts. The Dadaists, Surrealists, and other avant-garde movements had already anticipated this earlier in the century when they put together whimsical collages from Victorian magazines, newspaper clippings, and advertisements. And watch any old American cartoons and you'll see similar tongue-in-cheek citations of earlier cultural artifacts. Programs like "Looney Tunes" were using this maneuver already in the 1930s and transmitted this legacy to the burgeoning cartoon industry. In a Bugs Bunny cartoon from 1957 called "What's Opera,

Doc?" the animation is accompanied by Richard Wagner's music, including one bit in which Elmer Fudd sings "Kill the Wabbit" to the melody of "Flight of the Valkyries." Citation certainly has a much longer history than its twentieth-century iteration. It is perhaps rather a quantitative question; the farther one moves along in history, the more one has to cite, consciously or subconsciously. And as more and more possibilities of novelty are exhausted, the more one must rely on the past.

In the 1990s, there were two new television programs that modeled for spectators how to mock the media they beheld. Both shows involved the viewer watching another set of viewers making fun of old movies (in the case of *Mystery Science Theater 3000*) and music videos (in the case of *Beavis and Butt-head*). These programs prefigured the contemporary tendency to take almost all cultural production in jest and to mock in particular the cultural artifacts of our forebears.

The television show *Mystery Science Theater 3000* was a harbinger of the age of irony to come. This program, with a wide cult following, ran in the United States from 1988 to 1999 and consisted of a man (Joel, then later Mike) and his two alien friends (Tom Servo and Crow T. Robot) who sat in an empty movie theater forced to watch bad, mostly sci-fi movies from decades past. These movies, which really did exist, had titles such as *The Slime People*, *Robot Holocaust*, and *Earth vs. the Spider* and were played in their entirety to the impertinent trio, meant as torture imposed upon them by an evil scientist named Dr. Clayton Forrester. Instead of losing morale during the forced viewing of these bad movies, the three take them as a source of derisive fun. Spectators at home see their silhouettes, as if the protagonists sat before them in a movie theater, and listen as they make sarcastic joke after sarcastic joke, commenting on the horrible special effects, mocking the cheesy acting, pointing out the inconsistencies of the plot, making endless pop references, until the film's end, surviving happily and thus thwarting the evil scientist's nefarious scheme. It was not uncommon for the program to exceed four hundred jokes per ninety-minute episode. The show provided a kind of model for dealing with the aesthetic failures of preceding generations. This *mise-en-abyme*—spectators watching spectators watch a bad movie—created instant identification and a kinship between the sassy trio and the viewers at home. They were in essence the mouthpiece for our responses to poor aesthetic choices. However, the rational consequence of such mockery is the inevitable set of questions: "Have we ourselves produced anything better? Or does our generational contribution consist in merely reconfiguring all that has come before? Someday, won't we also be the object of ridicule by our descendants?" So the preemptive ironic maneuver came to bear.

Then, there were those two undesirables, Beavis and Butt-head. Born in 1993, they look like genetic mistakes, aborted doodles that made it out of the trash bin. They are sketchy in every sense of the word. With their rock T-shirts and hairless, string bean legs descending into white tube socks, Beavis and Butt-head go together like brothers from another ugly mother. Their ugliness is what was so delightful. Until their conception, the golden proportions of cartoon cuteness or heroism were the norm on TV. There were few if any undesirables to be found, and generally only as villains (Bluto, Gargamel, Skeletor, etc.). Beavis and Butt-head are ugly and coarse but relatively harmless, except to the frogs they use as baseballs and to the women they ogle as objects. Butt-head's gums are always showing, stippled with little inexplicable black dots. His braces are composed of single lateral lines across his little teeth. With squiggly eyebrows, flared nostrils, and an underbite, Beavis looks like a dumb, caffeinated fiend with puffy blond hair. Who could forget his alter ego Cornholio, whose face sticks out from the neck hole of his T-shirt while his arms are bent in right angles toward the sky? When they arrived on TV, there were probably few who, after watching them, successfully stifled the urge to imitate their throaty "huh uh uh uh" on the occasion of, well, almost anything at all. I admit that I incorporated their utterances into my everyday speech and used them whenever I could. Even now, their grunts seem the only proper responses to particular situations, functioning like the "That's what she said" phrase in the first decade of the 2000s. They always made me think a little of Bill and Ted, famous for their Excellent Adventure: all four of these non-gentlemen were slouchy, charmingly stupid, into rock music and babes, opposed to authority. These new models of masculinity replaced the classic archetypes: the international gentleman (James Bond); the suave, well-dressed man (Cary Grant); the young, mysterious rebel (James Dean); the wise old man (Mr. Miyagi); the bookish nerd (Steve Urkel); the muscles-and-guns guy (Rambo); and countless others. They made adolescent men feel comfortable in being how they already were. With Beavis and Butt-head, there was no longer the imperative to be a man of distinction or mystery, to be intelligent or ambitious. You could just be a dude. And part of being a dude was making fun of just about everything.

Beavis and Butt-head jeer at the people who share their cartoon world, like Coach Buzzcut, Principal McVicker, Daria, and Stewart, but they also provide sarcastic running commentary during music videos by all sorts of artists, such as Snoop Dogg, Björk, Megadeth, Rollins Band, and Devo. Yanni takes a particularly hard beating, as Beavis mistakes him for Geraldo Rivera and Butt-head calls him "the biggest butthole I've ever seen in my life." People have certainly always commented on the culture they consume while they're consuming it, but this framing illustrated how entertaining it could be to dissect culture in real time. It was a democratizing exercise; anyone could be a critic, not just Siskel and Ebert. Furthermore, it was free and could be used in nearly any circumstances. All that was needed was a source object; then the improvisational taunting could begin.

There were other early signs, too, of the ironic age to come, such as *The Simpsons*, which began in 1989, a cartoon designed mainly for adults. We now have a plethora of cartoons for grown-ups, like *South Park, Family Guy*, and the animated stuff on Comedy Central. Then, in 2000, the *Jackass* franchise began. One evening recently in a hotel, I was flipping through TV channels and noticed that on almost every channel, there was either a young guy doing stupid things or some kind of murder scenario, usually with a young, attractive, female victim. At first, I thought it had mainly to do with the time slot in which I was watching, but I tried it the next morning and came across a similar entertainment landscape. Dumb guys and dead girls. Most of the stereotyping on TV is as offensive to men as it is to women. So why do any of us accept the reductive handicapping of human potential on the screen? Maybe we want to see the worst possible versions of ourselves play out rotten lives in our stead so we can see hypothetically what our ugliest selves look like without actually living it.

As these early harbingers of widespread irony came to bear, the digital age arrived. The interactive nature of video games created a new kind of hypothetical living that allowed us to frame ourselves virtually, thus becoming part of the media itself. The Internet was largely responsible for the dissemination of the ironic posture modeled by shows like *Beavis and Butt-head* and *Mystery Science Theater 3000,* compounded by the subsequent comment culture of blogs and social networking sites. And there was an important cultural overlap that occurred in the '90s: the early days of widespread Internet and the emo movement. This overlap was significant. Emo was a kind of new Romanticism that revolved around the angst of the solitary subject whose primary medium of expression and identification was music. My Chemical Romance, Sunny Day Real Estate, Jimmy Eat World, The Get Up Kids: a whole slew of bands came to represent the movement. Emo adherents left a large archive of visual material that helps an outsider to understand the patterns of their aesthetic. I have a feeling they single-handedly popularized the selfie. Their black, side-swept bangs half covered their thickly lined eyes. Pale faces. Piercings. They were androgynous and forlorn and vaguely suicidal. So what happened when these young, melancholic souls made themselves vulnerable online, sharing self-portraits with despondent faces or revealing their suffering in words? They were met with scorn and ridicule. They were ripped to shreds, convicted before their trial. I think it is no coincidence that because the first instance of collective, digital vulnerability was met with collective bullying, people wised up very quickly. An unspoken law of Web behavior practically wrote itself: "He who maketh himself vulnerable online shall be made a mockery." Defenses were summarily raised. Compare the emo kid and the hipster kid: are they really so different? The main distinction is that the hipster is nearly impervious to criticism since she has already shielded herself with self-derision. The emo kid, a not-so-distant ancestor of the hipster, had journeyed into uncharted waters, only to be swallowed whole by the great white whale of contempt. Her descendants mastered what she had not: the art of concealment through self-ridicule.

What is the unofficial tone of the Internet today? Have a look at how those who were born and raised with it express themselves online. Look at Facebook, at Twitter, in the comments section of other popular sites. The language of middle-class Americans between the ages of, say, thirteen and thirty-five is dripping with irony. Photo comments in particular manifest heavy doses of the stuff, perhaps because the photo serves as a clear source object to which wit may be attached, like Beavis and Butt-head's music videos. Cleverness doesn't just come to life from out of nowhere; it needs a host to feed it. Comment culture in general provides the illusion that one has an actual voice. It is seen as an opportunity for original self-expression and the kind of giving of opinion that feels like a vote. But comments are lost in the great flurry of comments, which all resemble one another. I remember how depressed I was upon joining Facebook to see how very little deviation there was from a limited number of expressive patterns in people's posts, including my own. It was as though we'd all been programmed by the same person. Everything was dismally uniform. And despite the Internet's promise of the proliferation of marginalized voices, there sure is a lot of sameness on the Web. It feels like a sort of self-imposed, subconscious limitation, as though our social habitus had determined decades in advance everything we would type today.

One thing is certain: ironic living is a first-world problem. Could you imagine an ironic mustache in Bangladesh? Nerd glasses in Haiti? Goofy pseudojournalists delivering jokes between serious news reports in Somalia? Living conditions in these and many other places are simply not conducive to the self-indulgence of a life lived ironically. In America, the most irony-free places are those communities in which economic hardship imposes reality on everyday life. Go to the poorest neighborhoods in any town and it is unlikely you will find ironic frills. Instead, you will find minds preoccupied with more pressing problems. While it is true that irony can be used as an entertaining diversion, a way to distract the brain for a while from the toils of everyday life, it rarely saturates the lives of those who have to worry about making rent. It is not the first reflex when you can't afford health insurance. In some parts of the world, including certain regions and neighborhoods in the U.S., ironic living is not possible. There is simply not enough wealth, comfort, entertainment, or security.

My reflections on ironic living crystallized in a different kind of place: the hip Berlin quarter known as Neukölln. This area used to be the home of primarily Turkish families of modest means but has recently become a hipster Mecca, perhaps because of the low rent and the necessity of getting out of Kreuzberg, the former hippest spot in Berlin, due to

the tourist invasion there. By the time you read this, Neukölln will certainly already have been abandoned for more
fashionable waters. But there in the summer of 2012, between
reading chapters of Dostoyevsky's *The Idiot*, I looked out the
window at the throngs of hipsters, many of them American. The contrast between what I read and what I saw in
the streets could not have been more pronounced. The protagonist, named Prince Myshkin, is the idiot to whom the
title refers. The novel portrays him as a paragon of Christian
virtue who bears no trace of deception or duplicity. He is
incapable of lies and deceit, and embodies idealism and guile-
less beauty. There was a total incongruity between this protagonist and the ostentatious, self-obsessed throngs that filled
the bars beneath my window in Berlin. No Prince Myshkin
was to be found among them. Dostoyevsky wrote of him,
"In the very expression of his face this naïveté was unmistak-
ably evident, this disbelief in the insincerity of others, and
unsuspecting disregard of irony or humour in their words."
This exceptional quality makes him appear as an idiot to the
deceitful company he keeps; while members of his entourage spend their days engaged in social warfare, scheming
and conspiring against one another, Myshkin navigates their
world as a naive victim of their plots. No one believes that
he is sincere because it is inconceivable to them that a person
could live in such a way. I have often wondered if Dostoyevsky had the Italian stock theater character Pierrot in mind
when he created the figure of Prince Myshkin. Pierrot is the
obverse figure of Harlequin, that commedia dell'arte character I compared to today's deep ironist. Pierrot represents
substance and depth. His muse is the moon. He embodies
what is real, what is palpable, what contains the aura of pres-

ence. He is naive and trusting. In the French writer Michel Tournier's depiction, Pierrot is a humble baker who invests all of his care and warmth into baking a simple loaf of bread.

Prince Myshkin is absolutely devoid of irony and could serve as a model for non-ironic, non-defensive living. The world would be a dismal place if everyone behaved exactly like him; but I believe American society could function with less friction and with more depth if Myshkin were kept in mind as a model when people move through their daily lives. While Dostoyevsky's Myshkin incarnates Christian virtue, I would reconceptualize this model for our times as a post-Christian, and more specifically, post-religious figure. If we are to think of Myshkin as a practical model to live by in the contemporary age, we should embrace those aspects of his behavior and disposition that are not exclusive to Christianity, but that belong also to other faiths and to faithlessness, and are compatible with reason and common sense.

If you are reading this and are unfamiliar with *The Idiot*, I urge you to run—don't walk—to get a copy. This is not simply a plug from a literature professor for one of the greatest novels in history. (It is, a little.) I recommend this book because a possible antidote to excessive irony finds itself in this character, a metaphysically transparent human who lives in a world of masks. In each of his encounters with the ironic world, one feels the pull toward something more substantial, something less surface. He manages somehow to undo the opacity of the social world. The characters who come into contact with him are thrown off course by his forthrightness, even if he doesn't actually transform them and the story's end turns out to be an unhappy one. If you are vexed by the state of things, you have a responsibility to derail brainless habits and to be a human clinamen, that deflective force that sets things in motion. If you find the Great American Irony Binge to be intolerable, start with an active extraction of those ironic elements that reside in your speech, your clothing, your living space. Speak vulnerably. Behave vulnerably. Live vulnerably. And know in advance that the vultures will aim their hunger at you. This is the nature of the thing. The vulture lacks the imagination to think about how it feels to be dismembered.

The Latin *vulnerabilis* means wounding, injurious. That which is vulnerable is capable of being wounded. What does a vulnerable soul look like? The Japanese director Akira Kurosawa made a film adaptation of Dostoyevsky's novel in 1951. Have a look at the face of the actor Masayuki Mori in his role as the Idiot. One has the impression that he has simply taken off his skin and put his bare self forward. He is before you plainly in black and white, in the literal and figurative sense. You and the characters who interact with him are unnerved by the penetrative impact of his black stare. It stretches across the screen, unprocessed and unavoidable.

Myshkin is, of course, a fiction. But real life contains plenty of non-ironic models as well. Young children communicate with utmost sincerity, not yet having been indoctrinated into the social. They mean what they say and say what they mean. Up to a certain age, they cannot even detect the irony of adults; they take everything at face value. I'm not promoting some kind of forced naiveté or willful ignorance; rather, I think that the child is fortunate to be new to the ways of the world and capable of approaching them without assuming that an attack is inevitable. It would be refreshing to return to such a state, those early moments before the social world displayed its cruelties. Very small kids are certainly capable of duplicity, but it is usually the kind related to selfish needs of the body, not to demoting the dignity of others.

Recently, I was seated on an eight-hour flight to Berlin next to an unaccompanied six-year-old boy. The flight attendant asked me to keep an eye on him, to help him if he needed something to eat or drink, and to make sure he was fine during the flight. It took a while for our conversation to get started. I helped him put some cartoons on the screen in front of him. He chose some vintage Tom and Jerry. I was surprised that such a dusty old cultural artifact had found its way onto a transatlantic flight in 2013, but there was that old cat-and-mouse duo together again. It was one of my favorite episodes, the one where Tom somehow ends up conducting an orchestra. Jerry manages to lure ants onto the score from the opera *Carmen*, which Tom is using to conduct a song. The ants rearrange themselves frenetically, thus changing the composition and twisting Tom into acrobatic tangles as he tries to keep up with the lurching notes. "You know," I told the boy next to me, "this was on TV when I was a kid, too." He responded with one simple phrase: "Old people are funny." His response was jarring and perfect. Blunt, honest, and unintentionally amusing. He had not yet been tutored in the art of prettying things up for others. His statement wasn't meant as a hurtful critique, just as a plain declaration of the truth. As a woman "midway upon the journey of our life," as Dante put it, I actually am kind of old in comparison to a small human who hasn't even seen a full decade of this hairy planet yet. I liked this little guy already. And he made the trip even more enjoyable when he showed me a portrait he'd made of us sitting on the plane together, using rainbow colors on the screen in front of him.

A stone exhibits no sarcasm. Trees blowing in the wind do not require interpretation. And when we find animals funny, it is because we project upon them human characteristics and personalities. I saw a large bulldog the other day lying on his belly on the pavement, his legs splayed out flat in four directions. This looked absurd and I couldn't help but laugh. He stared at me from down there, not registering at all why I would find his posture laughable. What is a laugh to a dog? I had to ask myself what was funny about it and concluded that he'd taken up the position of a comically exhausted human who had just sprawled out on the floor. I wondered for a moment if dogs find it funny when humans imitate some canine gesture. Probably not. Although we would like to think we have true companions in this world outside our species, much of what we believe animals feel about us is a comforting self-delusion.

Irony dwells in the city and the suburbs, in the media and all things human made. But if you leave the human behind, there isn't irony anywhere. Sit at a creek and try to watch nature adopt a self-defensive ironic posture. Nature simply does not communicate in these terms. Any ironic reading of it, we put there. Soil, snow, deer, clouds, cacti, stars, minnows, algae, lava, ants: they are what they are. It isn't surprising that thinkers have pointed people toward nature as the place to escape the human. If you ever feel exhausted by the ironic buzz, you at least have the natural world as recourse. And if you go, get as far away as you can and abandon people and their useless accumulation of objects. Stay plain. Leave your devices and your accessories. Leave your name brands and your copyrights. Just an afternoon without any punch lines, any interpretive layers, any posturing. The sun doesn't snicker under its breath and the moon doesn't wear a trademark.

There are even more places to look for non-ironic models. A woman from Canada named Donna once wrote to me about her son, who has severe cerebral palsy. She explained eloquently how irony is completely absent from his behavior, and that she believes this to be a feature of the character of people with severe disabilities and their caretakers. Such people are bound to a rhetorically unembellished existence. She recalled hearing the famous neurologist Oliver Sacks say something like, "People with disabilities are condemned to always being themselves." This beautiful formulation gets at something essential: irony is a cultural prosthesis that has little to do with the intrinsic state of being a human animal. It is supplemental.

This gives us a couple of possible ways to look at irony: either as a frivolous mode of expression or as a sign of progress, a higher evolution of the human. If we take the first position, keeping Donna's son in mind, his life is somehow less frivolous and more bound to authenticity (an admittedly problematic word) than someone who can make silly smoke screens behind which to hide. He is what he is. What we see is what we get. There is no complex process of deciphering what he could really be meaning. In this way, irony takes us *away* from the essential. It adds distance between ourselves and the crux of being.

If we take the second position, one that depicts irony as a complex linguistic or semiotic process that requires high-order cognitive skills, then the failure of Donna's son to live ironically is evidence of an inferiority. It serves as a bench-mark for establishing a qualitative hierarchy among humans: those who know how to use irony are more advanced than those who do not. This fits with the first-world primacy narrative, does it not? If one takes this position and the examples I've given of ironic living as a first-world problem, then first worlders could get very self-congratulatory about their advanced cognitive ability. Furthermore, if one takes this second position, it assumes that people who do not use irony are somehow lesser beings. But if anything, our current ironic binge seems a sign of decline rather than progress. It represents a struggle with moderation, one of the many examples of our tendency toward excess.

What does each of these categories have in common: people with disabilities, people in economically challenging circumstances, children, nature? Other than their aversion to ironic living, each has been relegated to subhuman in various discourses throughout the centuries. In the hierarchy of who deserves more to thrive, the constituents of these categories have, in diverse sociohistorical contexts, been placed below others; more specifically, below the deciders who shape how a particular societal unit runs. I bring this up only in passing to underscore the layers of cultural complexity involved in the contemporary first-world problem of ironic living. It is not tied merely to aesthetics or rhetoric. It is bound up in all of the other untidy intricacies of people coexisting in the world. One can never make a clean break.

The word "sincerity" has been offered up as the opposite of, and perhaps the antidote to, "irony." The name most associated with the New Sincerity movement is that of David Foster Wallace. But is it ironic that the voice of New Sincerity committed suicide? I do not make light of this fact, nor am I suggesting that Wallace's suicide was not the direct result of the deep clinical depression that plagued him for years. But I do believe that a person committed to sincerity may often feel alienated in contemporary America and see no other way out of the ironic loop. As a pop-culture authority, Wallace was constantly exposed to ironic signals. Even his own writerly vocation was not safe; the contemporary writer takes a very big risk in choosing to write without irony. Wallace himself was certainly no stranger to ironic maneuvers in his pages, even if he did crave a more candid expressive economy between people. In short, the pull of ironic living is hard to resist. If you approach it neutrally, with no conscious will against it, it will likely lure you in. This goes back to my claim about our fluency in Ironese. This is the paradox of being a writer or filmmaker or musician in our time who hasn't yet passed middle age: if you adopt the language of irony, you can communicate with your own cohort but you can't change it; if you refuse the language of irony, your words fall upon deaf ears. Your message remains undeciphered and indecipherable.

What would an effective New Sincerity movement even entail? It seems that such an explicit campaign to alter people's behavior and modes of self-expression would be doomed to fail even before it began. I can think of no movement in history that so openly took people's affective lives into its hands and succeeded. One simply cannot police the expressive will of the human. Nor can one really convince it to change through reasoning, through suggestion, or through any other sort of appeal. I've come to terms with this, even though I can't resist using this essay to encourage cognizance of ironic living and to entertain alternatives to it. The truth is, we simply have to wait. Our species cannot be hurried toward its next cultural shift. On a constructive note, however, moments like the ironic one we're now experiencing are helpful as diagnostic tools for figuring out what's going on with the human. Society signals what it needs through culture. Civilization shows what it wants through the behavioral quirks of the people, through the trends and penchants of a given moment. Scrutinizing the symptoms of this moment, of our moment, help us to make a kind of psychogram of the collective brain.

Maybe just by noticing and describing the problem, public attention can be turned toward a slow solution. The hipster phenomenon has basically run its course, too mainstream to be cool any longer. When this movement is replaced by something else, the visible irony in the form of fashion will probably decrease, but it is difficult to say what irony's role will be in the next twenty years. While I would like to predict that the next big thing is a sweeping commitment to sincerity, I doubt this will happen. This thought is far too utopian and the poles too neatly diametrical. Will it be a period of cultural reassessment? A diagnostic moment before the beginning of a new ethos? Will the change happen as an explosion or as a whisper? Will people withdraw into themselves in quiet reflection? Will they raise their voices? Will they triple, quadruple, or quintuple the layers of irony with which they veil their speech? Will they develop a new, blunt means of expression? These completely unanswerable questions at least project us toward the future we will soon inherit. And they make us think inside and outside ourselves, inside and outside our cohort. As a Gen-Xer, I wonder how it must be to grow up in this environment today. What does it feel like to be in high school, for example, where your life is constantly available for comment online? Where your virtual existence perhaps trumps your real-life existence, at least socially? Young people have always been unkind to one another, but now the venues for unkindness have multiplied exponentially. Can you ever say how you really feel, using your own real name? Is there some kind of unwritten imperative that you target the weaknesses of others, like a reflex, while keeping your own defenses up at all times? Humans are adaptable and have found ways to cope with this new reality in which social surveillance sees everything. But these new material conditions are profoundly altering our affective response to others and compressing the visceral self into an ever-tighter bundle, lodged invisibly under thick sheaths of fiction. I shy intuitively away from all of today's necessary posturing, knowing all the while that if I were in high school now, I would probably just shut up and adapt. If I never knew any differently, maybe I wouldn't even be sad about it.

What is clear is that there's evidence everywhere that people are hungry for sincerity and directness. We want the freedom to be vulnerable. While the New Sincerity movement never really took off, the fact that the term "New Sincerity" even exists points toward a desire for the possibility of candid expression, received and given. Paradoxically, the place people feel most comfortable expressing themselves sincerely, albeit while remaining anonymous, is sometimes the Internet. You can never be sure that people are being straight with you, but you at least have the option to say what you really mean behind a curtain of anonymity. You have a forum for venting, for confessing, for criticizing. The steam you let off can pearl up on the Web. FML sites and others like Post-Secret allow people to communicate their frustrations, hang-ups, anxieties, triumphs, vices, embarrassments, hesitations, and the little joys and pains that make up daily life. These sites are insular havens for the modern disquieted soul.

Maybe the future of sincerity is the underground. Our entire lives might be digitized eventually, so it is heartening to see some seeds of sincerity embedded in the vast network that will carry us toward what we will become. In the end, maybe we will stop desiring sincerity with a signature on it and opt for the anonymous assortment. Unclaimed sincerity, here and there on the Web, when and where we want it. We can feel more human whenever we need to, without any risk. We can access a human signal when our heart desires it. Longfellow put it like this:

> Ships that pass in the night, and speak each other in
>   passing,
> Only a signal shown and a distant voice in the
>   darkness;
> So on the ocean of life we pass and speak one another,
> Only a look and a voice, then darkness again and a
>   silence.

I don't argue that irony should be eliminated from life. Rather, I would welcome a nuanced management of the ironic binge, a recalibration of our sensors, which have become overstimulated to the point of uselessness. In its sub-tler form, irony is not only potent, it is beautiful. When it's good, it gets to your core like desert lightning, turning sand to glass. And as a tool for the underdog or a means for social change, I can't put it on a high enough pedestal. When it's *for* something, irony has a richness and sophistication beyond description. And pinpointing exactly *how* it does what it does is included in the joy of beholding it. It turns into sky what was thought to be ground and then invites the study of how this reversal happened.

What point does today's ironic reflex attempt to get across? If it merely conveys a cynical message that nothing is stable any longer, that everything is relative, that what we believe in today will be annulled tomorrow, then I think we get it by now. There are scores of other ways to express or resist this state of affairs. This is not the first generation that has come to this conclusion. Imagine those who witnessed either of the world wars trying to make sense of life afterward. You get temporarily speechless and dumb, and then you un-numb and start walking again. Vitalist striving is a human compulsion. We've been trying the ironic reflex for a while, but it has begun to feel helpless, giving the human too little credit. As a brief suspension of faith in whatever, irony gave us a chance to rest a little, to get our bearings. The very act of posing the question, "What do we want next?" should fill us with anticipation, a soft giddiness for what is to come. This could be a collective turn toward sincerity or directness or the natural or the serious. It might involve a conscious self-training against narcissism or a cultivation of empathy. Maybe we will decide together to be temporarily silent.

The Patina of Things

I learned from *Antiques Roadshow* that you should never clean the patina off old objects you believe to be valuable. Doing so could reduce their value drastically. Leaving the patina alone is counterintuitive: one has the impulse to "Make It New," as Ezra Pound exhorted. But the new always gets old in turn, and aging cannot be forestalled.

Patina is a visible, material manifestation of history. It preserves the undisturbed biography of an object. A piece of bronze with a greenish cast proves that it has lived a long if not interesting life, exposed to the weathering of existence. Patina gives age and character to the object, a kind of personality. It also serves a protective function, offering a thin guard against the elements or pollutants in the air. It seals the object in time. By stripping off the patina, we expose the naked object to a coarse future. This is symbolic: experience in general offers a protective property. Experience—which is a combination of time and worldly contact—pads things, people, and places from what is to come.

My mother went through a phase when I was younger in which she painted objects in our house to make them look old. She would apply a thin layer of paint to, say, a wooden box with designs carved in it and then wipe the color away from the protruding parts of the surface so that paint remained only in the crevices. She was attempting to forge history, not in the sense of creating history but in the sense of faking it. I remember watching with fascination as she turned banal objects from the craft store into weighty, seemingly meaningful things. She accelerated their aging and gave them instant gravitas. It was so easy to turn objects solemn! She breezed through the house, aging every crevice she could find, making our house sag with the weight of the ages.

Time knows how to get into the crevices of things. This is where history resides: in the creases of material culture. But patina, and thus history, can be found in nonmaterial culture as well, in speech, in music, in ideas. It is the marker of experience. Patination requires time and exposure to real, blunt existence. It cannot be rushed.

Now we want to strip the patina off everything, an impulse that denies time and experience their integrity. People can tolerate aging and the aged only in small and carefully administered doses, like a two-week tour of European castles or a visit for an afternoon to Grandma in the rest home. History is too heavy in comparison to the radiance of youthful faces and gadgets fresh off the assembly line.

Paradoxically, there is a simultaneous rush to convert current events into past ones. We want to change the old into the new and, at the same time, we try to change the new into the old. This takes many forms. Sometimes, oldness comes in handy for conveying stately authority or meaningful nostalgia. When the old is needed, American culture has a ready solution, something akin to my mother's painting technique. Where there is no oldness, no authority, no history, we try to add a new, fresh layer of artificial old through Instagram filters, new clothing made to look vintage, and the museumification of random objects. This attempt to make life instantly significant without the burden of time and experience ultimately feels hollow. Authority cannot be had just like that. I believe people intuitively know this, whether they are cognizant of the fact or not. For whatever reason, they seem willing to accept counterfeit authority as the real thing.

This desire to make the new into the old has to do with an impatience for history to arrive. Do we envy the Europeans, with their surplus of history? Do we think that by rushing our own stories, we can somehow accumulate history faster and catch up to them? This same impatience makes news organizations rush to be the first to deliver the most breaking news before their competitors, which leads them in many cases to report absolutely false information. Instead of breaking news, we get broken news. The same impatience explains the popularity of Twitter, which gives us a minute-by-minute account of the lives of people we find interesting. We don't want the information secondhand from some tabloid. We want the details now, directly from the source, in a digestible morsel. We want to watch our autobiography write itself.

And then there's the more pervasive desire to make the old new again. When people get plastic surgery or fetishize youth by altering their bodies in some way, they are essentially removing their own patina. They want to strip away the evidence of experience. They wish to remain babes with powdered bottoms, fresh as the morning dew, spared from the weariness of the world. However, the most interesting people I've ever met had the most patina. Wrinkly people are awesome. The same goes for people with scars and grey hair. People who sag or are bent with age have stories to tell through their bodies. Foxes are wonderful; silver foxes are divine. Crow's-feet are just about the most attractive feature the human face can have. And laugh lines . . . what ill can be said of laugh lines, those striated traces of joys and pleasures, past and present? I will welcome wrinkles someday as signs of a life fully and properly lived. Jorge Luis Borges wrote a beautiful passage that gets exactly at this in the afterword of his 1960 book *El Hacedor* (*The Maker*):

> A man sets out to draw the world. As the years go by, he peoples a space with images of provinces, kingdoms, mountains, bays, ships, islands, fishes, rooms, instruments, stars, horses, and individuals. A short time before he dies, he discovers that the patient labyrinth of lines traces the lineaments of his own face.

The wrinkle is a token from Dama Fortuna to remind you how long you've been allowed to spend time among the living. The wrinkle is a biological badge of longevity.

A Frenchman once said something very interesting to me. He said that when you live in Europe, you are surrounded at all times by the visible history of your country, particularly in the large capitals where the old architectural heritage is on display. However, when he traveled to the U.S. for the first time, he had nowhere to look for history. The past was at first invisible to him. True, there are some American cities with preserved buildings from the 1600s, but this is the exception and not the rule. Almost everything here is relatively new. (I smile when I see a sign outside a U.S. store: IN BUSINESS SINCE 2001! The Weihenstephan Brewery in Bavaria was founded in 1040 and is still in operation.) In Europe, it is not uncommon to stumble upon a church that was built before Columbus even "discovered" America. You've probably heard an American say about Europe, "There's just so much *history* there," as if we somehow had less of it. This is absurd. As far as I understand it, each continent is more or less equally old. Why does history only count if it takes a visible, preferably architectural or textual, form? In the U.S., evidence of indigenous history was basically annihilated, so what was left? Nature. My French friend continued his observation by saying that the only old, visible history in the United States consists of mountains, old-growth forests, and rivers and lakes. The natural world is the single visible thing that has been in place for a very long time and which constitutes a kind of nonanthropocentric history. The contours of the land and the oldness of the woods then are our uniquely American patina.

So, in the spirit of *Antiques Roadshow* counsel, I offer a piece of friendly advice for preserving the intrinsic value of the buildings, bodies, and natural wonders of the New World: don't touch the patina.

On Distraction

Clever gimmicks of mass distraction yield a cheap soulcraft of addicted and self-medicated narcissists.

—CORNEL WEST, "Dr. King Weeps from His Grave"

Everything in the Big Bang universe tends toward dispersal: families, culture, languages, ideas. Life seems centrifugally oriented, fleeing its center. People leave home, culture gets hybridized and diffuse, words get ever more distant from their roots, and the mind moves relentlessly toward new inventions, new possibilities, leaving the old behind. Yet there remains an inner longing for some original state, a hunger for the seed. Is it existential homesickness? Primordial nostalgia? Phantom limb longing? Womb hunger? Root sickness? In America, the land of mutts, we are centerless. Despite efforts to forge a national mythology, it never holds its form. Upon seeing the brilliant, raucous rainbow splash of accents, languages, colors, classes, temperaments, and lifestyles that we embody today, the ghosts of our Founding Fathers would most certainly ask for a paternity test.

And with the progressive virtualization of daily life, a new phase of centerlessness has begun. We live in a state of distraction. The word "distract" means to pull apart in different directions, to draw and quarter the mind. In essence, it is a dissipation of the human. If I invest myself in ten simultaneous tasks, I send off my energies—mental and physical—along ten divergent paths. This conflicted diaspora leaves me disoriented. I have no place. I am atomized, divided eventually into my smallest components and sent off who knows where. Between the national deficit of attention and the financial deficit, I'm not sure which is the more pressing problem. Perhaps the first led to the second, as we were too distracted to notice the funny business going on with our money. Or maybe the gravity of these economic woes has sent us toward our slack-jawed screen gazing, an extended commercial break from the fiscal drama that plays on the screen called our lives.

So we've broken ourselves down into molecules, tossed this way and that. The mind is asked to disperse itself, often in competing directions. Even as I write this now, I keep drifting into and out of attention to my page. I am an unfaithful thinker. My mind keeps cheating on my text, checking out other thoughts, looking other daydreams up and down with desire. Oh, brain, thou lustful organ! Your harem of ideas is never large enough; you want to possess all the thoughts at once, dying in the arms of one idea while kissing the lips of another. *Libidinosa cerebrum!* Concentrate thyself!

I've begun to believe that dispersal is the intrinsic state of things. Migration, pollination, nomadism, erosion, the spraying of sperm, a river delta, satellites flung toward space, propulsive winds scattering sand and seed: all of these phenomena involve matter moving elsewhere from its place of origin. While one could spin out countless other examples of dispersal, it is less easy to list things that return naturally to their place of origin after they've left it. What if the whole point of the universe is merely to spread out? This could be the logic of the entire thing: a cosmos whose unique purpose is to dilate, to pulse outward, repeating its pattern on a microscopic level and on a grand scale as wide as the swelling universe. If this is the case, *Homo sapiens* participates readily in The Great Dispersal. This is the restless species that came up with the idea of saddling other species in order to get around faster. The human strives to quicken its pace on land, air, and sea. It points its telescopes at distant galactic objects and makes them destinations. The homebody exists in the human species as a type, but the desire to stay home—on an everyday basis and as an obstinate refusal to leave one's town of origin—verges on pathology. The one who stays at home is a doleful recluse, a persona non grata. Today, these pathetic souls find consolation and fellowship in faraway lands accessed through the virtual portal. Even at home, we are sedentary travelers.

Distraction is a metaphor that spatializes the mind. If distraction means "a state of being pulled apart," the mind is depicted as a kind of divisible unit whose composite parts can be torn asunder. Think of other metaphors used to describe this state of mind: "My mind drifted off." "I was lost in my thoughts." "I was off somewhere." "My head was in the clouds." "Sorry, I'm out of it." "Whoa, I just spaced out for a second." These metaphors work weirdly; considered in a bundle, the mind is attracted toward the boundless ether and the brain itself is a microcosm in which the human floats. You are an actor in the cosmic play staged inside your own skull. When you lose track of time and begin to daydream or enter a state of distraction, you either get lost somewhere inside your head or you move upward and away from your own body, toward the great beyond. Is this the pull of the universe, exerting its force on your mind? Are your efforts at concentration a mere resistance of the cosmic lure? Should you give in to this force greater than you and let your attention wander where it will? Or is the human mind one of the few instruments capable of real choice in the universe? Perhaps the universe, too, was tired of spreading itself thin and engineered the human mind as the hook on which it could catch itself.

Distraction is an internal static, a form of self-interference. The opposite of an analgesic—like ibuprofen, which relieves pain but keeps you conscious—it kills pain by smothering consciousness. Distraction sedates, dulling the sharp edges of life. If one's brain is numbed by the influx of images and sounds, by the flood of obligations, by the flurry of memos, one has an automatic alibi against a more real connectedness with people. Distraction provides the pretense for a less-than-superlative investment in any given relationship or other kinds of social contact. Busyness is an excuse, a way to sidestep others, even those we actually care about. A bit of joy is had in turning on whichever device, that portal that siphons the mind away from the here and now, that doesn't ask us explicitly for anything except to behold it. This makes immediacy less and less easy to handle. What is in front of us is unbearably real, with its insistent materiality from which it is uncomfortable to shy away. There is no possibility of delaying our response to it. The real just waits. Increasingly, human interaction without a filter verges on the painful because the skills in dealing with others face-to-face have been abandoned for the refinement of digital social skills. All communicative occasions today are ideally set up to avoid that horror of the modern soul: awkwardness.

The screen takes the pressure off these social situations, or at least buys a little more time to figure out how to approach them discreetly. Remote, mediated things are better than those that look us in the face because the distance in between acts as a buffer, softening the point of contact. Articulating our convictions in real time without the possibility of editing them is now intimidating. What if something comes out the wrong way? We've all transformed into ghosts of J. Alfred Prufrock, petrified by the potential faux pas that will leave us "pinned and wriggling on the wall." Who would volunteer to be the awkward insect? Perhaps if our wholeness of presence is in a single spot, we are easier to catch. It is for this reason that self-dispersal is preferable to self-concentration. We want to remain slippery, unbound. By investing less into one moment, into one friend, into one lover, into one job, into one task, into one life trajectory, we will be less wounded if we fail at this single pursuit. We can merely start up again with another of our half efforts.

I once caught a glimpse of the boy from Ipanema. I sat in the New York subway, hands in my lap, with my standard camouflage of plainness. In cities, I try as hard as possible to be as unremarkable as the pavement or a garbage can. This invisibility secures me the conditions for my favorite activity: people watching. Not an invasive, stalkerlike voyeurism, but the anthropological gaze of a person curious about other people. I like to study. So I sat there, imperceptible, watching people come and go, not talking of Michelangelo but texting of trifles and trivia. And as I sat there, a beautiful man walked in. A man of animal appeal and grace, who got everything stirring: the pheromonal, the circulatory, the respiratory, the salivary, the glandular, the cerebral. He was an ocular gift. In the history of human culture, it is mostly the beautiful woman walking by who has been rendered immortal through literature, music, and art. From Dante watching Beatrice pass with the Tuscan women, to Baudelaire's urban female passerby, to the girl from Ipanema . . . the woman walking by as we watch is an immemorial topos. But what about the man walking by? Someone surely would have written a poem about this one had they seen him. Michelangelo would have invited him to his studio. Did anyone else see him or was he a figment of my imagination? I looked to my right, then to my left . . . and felt trampled. I had no ally. I had no coconspirator. I had no interlocutor with whom to share this brutally beautiful spectacle. Everyone around me was looking at their phones. And then he got off the train. They just didn't see.

The distracted person has a look. As you talk to her, her eyes go elsewhere, to a cobweb in the corner—Does the spider who built it still live there?—or to some blank spot in the room that invites her to project upon it her mental film. On that featureless spot, she casts various tableaux of her real and imagined life unsequentially. She travels through time, tripping from the e-mail she got an hour ago, to that one trip she made to Ohio with some boyfriend (she's not sure which one), to the white shorts of Jack Tripper from *Three's Company*, to the melody of that Morphine song "Let's Take a Trip Together." Nothing feels linear. It feels rather like a very large painting whose visual components can be viewed only in small bits at a time. Everything is simultaneously present, but our organ of access can get to it only in pieces. She looks on, but her eyes are only occasionally living. They keep dying, turning ashen, glinting with sparks of life at irregular intervals, but they're basically dead. She has left waking life for the half-light arabesques of inner consciousness.

This is the lymphatic form of distraction, sluggish and dull. The sanguine form involves the distracted mind in a frenzy, full of blood and dynamism, with an adrenaline heartbeat and sweaty palms. I know someone whose plate is always brimming with responsibilities. Her hourglass empties at least thrice as fast as mine. Sometimes we sit together, having entered into the implicit contract of a conversation, a binding agreement which she breaches at regular intervals. The siren call of her not-so-smart phone runs her aground. When we both notice that her purse is vibrating, I lock her eyes with mine and test her. It is a test of sheer will. Whom will she pick? Her distant caller or me? I joust with this invisible windmill foe. It probably isn't even a call, probably just a text, an automatic alert from her bank or some such nonsense. Could you imagine back in the remote twentieth century if the mailperson delivered your letters, flyers, or bills to you wherever you happened to be sitting? What if postman Mr. McFeely showed up to hand-deliver each of your e-mails wherever you happened to be? His presence would begin to comfort you and you'd start to long for his visits. Where is he? It's been twenty minutes and I've gotten nothing. Why does Mr. McFeely tarry? I wish I could empty her hours to give her the luxury of focus. If the industrial age sought to empty time by dreaming up machines that could do our work for us, the digital age has refilled it with binary chores and entertainments that leave few hours vacant. What will be the features of third millennial time? The speed and distraction of this age create an unsustainable irritation. But will we ever again be attracted to slowness and focus? I think so. The ability of computers to play much faster than a human drummer has not done away with the need for slow-tempo acoustic ballads. The zippy journalism of today has not kept people from picking up thick novels. The sanguine form of distraction brought about by dispersive technologies will undoubtedly begin to bother us like a nervous wasp tapping at the window with its body, trying to be let in. It is too high-strung an experience, too full of sting.

In a scene from the rock opera *Jesus Christ Superstar*, Jesus wanders into a leper colony. The lepers, dressed in dark, shredded clothes, limp toward him looking for a miracle as the electric guitar accelerates and their pleas to be healed become ever more urgent. They crowd in on him, eventually overwhelming the small man as he shouts out from the mass of bodies that suffocate him, "There's too many of you! Don't push me! There's too little of me! Don't crowd me! Leave me alone!" You may feel this way at times, but no one will found a religion around your self-dispersal.

The book: a locus of focus. We apologists of the humanities haven't always done the best job of justifying our vocation, but it seems to me that the book is the best place for our case to make itself. The humanities—and, more specifically, literature and philosophy—demand a slow focus left out by many other progress-oriented disciplines like business and the sciences. In our field, the kinds of books that occupy the mind cannot be speed-read. If they are, which happens often in today's administrativersity, their real purpose is more or less elided. The texts we read are meant to take people out of the flow of time and muster their spread attentions into a tight bundle. This is the value of the humanities, whose teachers and students are trained in the art of deep attention. I have taken courses in which an entire week was spent discussing a single poem. For a captain of industry, this must sound like a ludicrous waste of time. In the deceptive game of equivalencies, this lost week equals a week of missed moneymaking, a week that could have been spent doing something that shows its output immediately and tangibly. But committing oneself earnestly to one page, to a few lines of verse, is one of the obvious ways left to fuse the eyes and brain in a crystal chorus. This enterprise dismisses the scale of useful equivalencies. Poems are made for us to spend time with them, to thread our thoughts through them like yarn through cat's cradle fingers, into and out of the holes in each letter. Imagine the kind of mental weaving made possible through a haiku like this one from Masaoka Shiki:

> Green shadow-dances . . .
> See our young banana tree
> Patterning the screen.

You and the poem commiserate outside of time. The complexity or simplicity of the ideas is nearly irrelevant; all that matters is the summoning text to which you affix your eye. The same can be done with a well-crafted piece of music, which invites close listening. Or a painting. What other fields rely upon slow focus as much as the humanities? As I'm sitting here, writing about the careful attention toward books, songs, and sculptures, a mourning dove has just landed on the roof across the way to remind me that nature itself is an open invitation to contemplative focus. His song is still a song; his body an image. This dove, in rose brown, just took me out of time in his own way and drew my eye toward him like a great verse. And now, he just slid down and away from his perch, a black-and-white flicker in his tail. A haiku about him:

> There, a mourning dove
> Became his own verse, lightly
> Sliding from his perch.

You may have noticed of late that the zombie has become a pop culture favorite on the little and big screens of TV and cinema. They're ugly and they're coming for us. As the Caribbean Marxist Frantz Fanon wrote, "Zombies, believe me, are more terrifying than colonists." The ubiquity of the undead today is not arbitrary. Cultural patterning is never arbitrary; it is always symptomatic. The fear of becoming the living dead has arisen because they surround us every day. They ride the train with us, bump into us on the street, stand in line with us at the grocery store. These soulless corpses are so distracted by their devices that they nearly forget there is a world other than the virtual one in which they've invested their full selves. The zombification of America manifests itself in the everyday collisions or near collisions of two, or three, or five people staggering down the sidewalk toward the impact point like badly programmed automatons. They are Roombas with a nervous system. At one time, the fusion of man and machine was imagined as an upgrade of human capacity, an improvement on the bodily limitations of the lowly *Homo sapiens.* The reality of *Homo digitalis* more closely resembles that of the humans from *Wall-E* than that of *Robo-Cop.* You may recall that the humans in Wall-E's world are listless and chubby, having lost the muscle mass to even walk. They sit in floating chairs and guzzle Big-Gulp-like beverages all day long while screens hover endlessly in front of their entertained faces. (When I saw this movie in the theater, I had the uncanny experience of looking toward the audience stuffing its collective face with twenty-dollar vats of popcorn and swigging from drink cups the size of cremation urns as they stared at their computer-generated doppelgängers doing the exact same thing.) Like the zombie, the new digital people are mobile but clumsy. They are alive but cold. They want to spread their own malady. (You've witnessed the scenes of social pressure to buy the slightly modified version of a nearly identical apparatus.) They want to devour the human brain.

There are few vignettes more depressing than that of the distracted collective. A family of four enters the restaurant and sits at the table next to me. Before the server even brings water for them, they've pulled out their screens and teleported their attentions elsewhere. For the duration of the meal, they barely speak; a bi-syllabic or tri-syllabic grunt escapes here and there. The server becomes merely a human interruption, an annoyance ripe for deletion were he not bringing the meal, which is summarily photographed and shared. They stare at the screens, punctuating their finger surfing with a bite here and there. The bill comes, they pay and shuffle out, the teenage son almost knocking over a tray full of food because he is not paying attention as he walks, his head bent downward toward his device.

Some predictions: The idea of family will dissipate as pets replace children and spouses. People will begin to adopt higher-order primates so they can have a pet that resembles a human but who won't argue or take up too many emotional gigabytes. (We will largely express ourselves through computing metaphors.) Screen zombification will come to represent borderline poverty and low culture, just as fast-food consumption does now. The well-off will have figured out a way to free themselves from their digital chains. Our future zombies will avail themselves of all of the latest technologies for the sake of convenience and efficiency. They will never be without their fluid pouch of coffee or some energy drink suspended from a rolling stand for intravenous delivery directly through the arm. By then, you will have stopped asking them questions or addressing them in any way; their headphones prevent them from hearing your voice anyway. They may have even plugged up all of their holes so as not to receive any external stimuli at all. By then, the images will be delivered directly to the occipital lobe via Wi-Fi. Then life will be composed entirely of distraction, one big and busy intake of peripheral information. Anything that pulls concentration away from the meaningful programming that will undoubtedly fill the rich hours of zombie leisure will be condemned. This includes sunlight, forests, conversation, and weekends reading quietly in a hammock.

As I'm pondering the notion of concentration, I realize I have no idea why concentration camps are called what they are. I dig a bit and find out. The idea was to isolate people into a manageable unit, to concentrate the "undesirables" in one spot. Under those circumstances, dispersal was seen as dangerous because surveillance and control would have been impossible unless everyone could be contained in a small area. The concentric circles, more hellish than Dante's, became small (the ghettos) then smaller (the camps) then smallest (the gas chambers or ovens). The current dispersal of information and people and goods across the planet could explain the paranoid drive to track every phone call and e-mail, to catalog people into an administrative framework that tries to contain them. This kind of containment or concentration or incarceration never wins against dispersal. When will we accept the idea of a free-range human?

Most countries—contemporary America in particular—are confronted by a common dilemma: should power be distributed evenly throughout the nation or should it be centered in one place, a central nervous system where the big decisions are made? There are compelling arguments for and against the concentration of power. The pros: a centralized system allows—in theory—for more uniform legislation, a smoother flow of resources, and a standardization of things like the tax code and civil rights laws. The cons: a single center of power cannot accommodate the great diversity of political and social interests state to state, and if something happens to the nerve center, everything falls apart. Some think that the individual states should deal with domestic problems and the federal government should take care of international ones. Some want to do away with the federal government altogether. The most interesting aspect of this problem is the way a diaphanous and international network—the Internet—has woven itself into life, tangling the categories of local and national. These terms mean less and less. So the problem of the concentration or dispersal of power may have answered itself. Power will be spread, densely, in a place called nowhere.

In 2010, I hid a short story I wrote in a drawer and left it there. This was a public service, honestly. The story was too wild and too self-aware; it wanted to say too much in too few pages. It was about the dispersal of digital images as an allegory for the dis-uniting of the United States after the Civil War. Its overzealous title is "We Became Ones and Zeros: An Allegory of Post–Civil War Reconstruction"; I felt the need to be explicit about its veiled meanings. This tale, full of mysticism, was about a woman who tries to retrace every photo that has been taken of her in her lifetime, even those taken by strangers when she wandered into their photos on the street, at tourist attractions, and in other arbitrary places. While the story was set in contemporary America, I slipped in a lot of language about the impossibility of reconstruction after the Civil War's end in 1865. The protagonist's impractical image quest was just a pretext for thinking about bigger impossible projects, like a true synthesis of North and South. I actually believe that the Civil War never really ended, that after its official denouement, the United States disintegrated—if it was ever actually integrated—into a cloud of discordant particulates, seeming at times to gather themselves into logical categories like "North," "South," "Black," "White," "Rich," and "Poor," but remaining ultimately an indistinct haze. Our nation took on a granular consistency, sand thrown thither. I chose the proliferation of images in contemporary life as a vehicle for my Civil War allegory for a good reason. With the advent of photography, many believed that the soul was stolen when one's photograph was taken. If we still believed this today, as our likeness is blown all over the planet in a digital flurry, this would mean that our soul, too, has been pulled to ribbons. I was trying to get at the idea that the nation's soul was shredded in the Civil War, that it was tattered to bits like penny paper, that it suffered from the same dissipation that is the general condition of contemporary life in America today. We are nothing but dispersal. Nothing but distraction. Dust before we even die.

History is cumulative. Civilization amasses all of its accomplishments through time, forgetting things here and there along the way, but ultimately dragging along behind it a big ol' potato sack chockfull of inventions, disasters, ideas, objects, decorations, steamships, and presidencies. So, asks a hypothetical naïf, shouldn't the contemporary human know more than the ancestors? In truth, we know less than our forebears, particularly when it comes to the basics like surviving in the wild. If you had to start over from scratch today, with no help from anyone—no books or tools at your disposal—would you know how to harness electricity? How to construct a weatherproof hut? How to build a flushing toilet? If you are a survivalist prepared for the apocalypse, you may be reading along smugly, confident that you would outlast most of the technocrats and yuppies. But the trade-off is that you have spent your life living in fear.

We could think both qualitatively and quantitatively about the accumulation of knowledge. The average person today probably has just as many or more bits of information in her mind as a specialist of theology in the Middle Ages would have had. But what is the *nature* of this information? Is it scholarly? Practical? Philosophical? Much of our knowledge today is chatter, mere gossip involving some celebrity, a firm grasp of this or that TV series plotline, or some product's features, arbitrary factoids about the most insignificant matters. With distinct roles in society, we each have little pieces of the civilizational puzzle. We are the builders, the administrators, the inventors, the consumers, the cleaners, the teachers. You're all tangled up in society, even if you can't actually identify a particular skill you possess, even if you do nothing but eat and watch TV. The point is, the abundance of all this worldly stuff and the progressive, fine-tuned articulation of specialized fields have meant that our own piece of the puzzle has grown much smaller over time. What it is *possible* to know has grown exponentially while our capacity to know has remained relatively stable. We've been piggybacking off the work of our ancestors, piling up more and more collective experience and things, and with the explosion of information technology, we've suddenly been faced with a much clearer and overwhelming picture of how little one person can know in the grand scheme of things. There's simply too much. Still, something compels us to know a little something about everything, and some of us feel guilty that we don't know enough. Is it better to know a little about a lot of things or a lot about a few things? Or is total ignorance the only bliss still possible? What advice would Doctor Faustus give us from his toasty little pit?

Remember the Renaissance man, that one guy who knew how to do everything? He goes by other names: the polymath, *Homo universalis*, the jack of all trades, the dilettante. The figure of the humanist, in its broadest sense, could fit in this list as well. The Renaissance man knew about aesthetics and math, he knew how to build rudimentary devices that worked, he knew something about the mechanics of the stars, he thought about friendship. A little of this, a little of that; he dismissed compartmentalization. The question, "Now, what do you do exactly?" at a cocktail party would have given him reason for pause.

Today, there is a tendency for people to hyphenate themselves vocationally or recreationally: Dre of N.W.A. fame is now a purveyor of titanic-scale headphones; Tilda Swinton is an actor, performance artist, and model; Brian May, the Queen songwriter and guitarist, has a Ph.D. in astrophysics. Everyone needs to be a part-time philanthropist, a part-time spokesperson, a vocalist-model-acrobat-belly dancer-poker-player. This kind of distraction of self is perhaps most visible in the push for children to participate in every conceivable extracurricular activity so as not to miss out on some experience their parents had, or so that their applications to college will be plumply padded by the time they graduate from high school. These kids, whose parents shield them from boredom at all costs, live in a world of entertainments and abstractions, activities for activities' sake that will indoctrinate them well into the cult of the busy. More and more, they are amputated from the real. The French philosopher Simone Weil was already lamenting this back in the 1940s when she wrote: "A lot of people think that a little peasant boy of the present day who goes to primary school knows more than Pythagoras did, simply because he can repeat from rote memory that the earth moves round the sun. In actual fact, he no longer looks up at the sky." These little kids are partitioned off as monarchs of their own small, fictional kingdoms where trophies are handed out like Halloween candy. So little Mackenzie believes she is a burgeoning genius by age nine because she made the honor roll three times in a row, came in first at a dance competition, knows all the lyrics from Taylor Swift's album *Red*, and showed her mom how to use Photoshop. You should have seen her at her second-grade graduation. She was *adorable*.

Are we Renaissance people or "jacks of all trades, masters of none"? The answer is obvious. How can little Mackenzie be shaken from her conviction that she is gifted, that she is wise beyond her years, that all of her energies and pluriform endeavors should be channeled toward crafting a flawless CV, the paper effigy of herself? Who will tell Mackenzie that her nation is in decline, that almost everything around her is a distraction from what is really at stake in civilization, that she has been fooled into believing she is a Renaissance person and not a self-important, foggy-headed robot whose assigned role is to consume products and images? There are undoubtedly a handful of authentic Renaissance people around who have a clear sense of the living connections between things concrete and abstract. But why should this kind of person be the exception and not the rule? Everything we need is at our disposal. We are more informed and equipped than ever to synthesize what we can see and what we can't, to think in terms of a whole rather than a pile of fragments. Nothing is ever really disjointed. Everything and everyone has its place in the subtle reticulation of existence, in its domesticated form (civilization and everything touched by it) and in its undomesticated form (stuff left unbothered by people). So it isn't a question of striving to understand the whole of it (that's impossible), just of acknowledging the fact that the whole exists. The true Renaissance person is endowed with panoramic attention. The habit of noticing the ensemble of everything and its constituent parts is a matter of will, not of innate aptitude. It involves the conscious noticing of things and the gaps that separate and connect them.

My mom describes a nightly experience for her, one I know well myself. It happens when her body is horizontal but her mind wants to stay vertical. She can't shut off the multitasking reflex, the one that wants to keep drafting new to-do lists, the one that throws in the face of the stars all the hypothetical scenarios of what tomorrow will look like, all the things left undone from the day before, and the worst-case scenarios of professional and personal life. She cannot power down her mind.

The unused energies from the day emit themselves in nocturnal life. So you can be distracted even in your sleep, if you can fall asleep at all. The nerves get you at night, whether you lie there gazing at the ceiling, which has become a cinema of tension (a double feature starring your angst), or whether you slide into a restless, staticky dreamscape with sharp, electric shocks biting at your ankles as you try to run from tomorrow. You are a human lightning rod for the agitation in the air.

There is a whole industry dedicated to tranquilizing (what a gentle, violent word) the nervous first worlder. Fragrant essential oils, melatonin, autogenic training, the hardcore prescription stuff, breathing exercises, yoga, recordings of soothing sounds (waterfalls, ocean waves, gentle rain), meditation, alcohol, weed: something for everybody. But the restless mind still disregards whether it is night or day. It is diurnal and nocturnal.

Our society does a particular disservice to women when it comes to distraction. All sorts of techniques have been mobilized to keep you from thinking through what is really at stake for women in the political and social landscape. For example, from childhood, women are indoctrinated to think of themselves in terms of how they appear to others. "You are so cute," the young girl is told. As she gets older, she becomes beautiful or pretty (or, in the worst case, she becomes ugly and thus irrelevant). She is taught to invest in products that will maintain and accentuate this prettiness. She can only see herself in the second degree, through the eyes of someone else. Magazines, TV, the Internet, and all those around her insist that her priorities remain in the realm of the aesthetic. She is allowed to be intelligent, but she must apologize for this intelligence by staying beautiful, or "taking care of herself," as the brutal euphemism phrases it. Walking down the street, listening to the radio, watching TV, surfing on the Internet: there is no place where she can let her thoughts pursue their intellectual course without the distracting assaults of manipulative advertising, let alone walk down the street and maintain an inner reflective monologue without some dude offering an unsolicited assessment of her assets. Even when she's waiting for the bus, the lingerie ad on the bus stop pulls her out of her critical thoughts to remind her that she'd better make looking good her priority or she'll spend her life alone. All this wrong-way pull means lots of cultural and political things can be gotten away with behind her back as she is drawn to think wistfully of her waistline. Distraction becomes addiction. We should all slip thick black markers into our pockets, handy for muffling out the loud garbage pictures that injure our sisters (and our brothers) in the public space. This is a favor to yourself, regardless of who you are.

Things aren't much better for men. For them (more specifically, straight men, who enjoy a certain privilege in consumerist culture; your desires rank high), distraction comes in the form of easy eroticism, which pokes relentlessly at those parts of your brain that respond to sex. Think of your scrotum as the coin purse that marketers hope to access. Unless you go out into nature or live in hermitic solitude, you have nowhere to look if you want to leave your biology aside for an afternoon and just think deeply about something. The boobs are ever more bouncy, the behinds ever more taut. Photoshop, the paroxysm of perfection, lets you pretend that flawless skin and golden proportions are a real thing. There is always someone willing to look into a camera with a lustful gaze to make you believe she wants you, *specifically you*. She makes you forget that a million men are recipients of the same, secretly indifferent gaze. How can you collect your thoughts when the temptress unfurls her bodily riches before you, slipping her covetous fingers into your wallet while you're distracted? Your own body, your own sexuality is used against you to keep you from realizing the fiction of the whole scene. But don't fall for it: it's a booby trap. I have a sneaking suspicion that the next phase in the exploitation of men will be a marketing move to pathologize male desire. After getting men stirred up with sexual, consumption-inducing imagery, which keeps them constantly bothered and restless, a medical cure for this ungovernable desire will surface. The ad will go something like this: "Hey, guys! Tired of being distracted by your horniness? Tired of your penis getting you into unpleasant situations? Try FDA-approved Penilax! It will calm edginess, increase focus and rationality, and save you the hassle of lawsuits, jail time, divorce, expulsion, bar fights, sexual harassment charges, hours of porn consumption and chatting, and general societal disapproval. Penilax: Give Yourself Some Scrotal Solace." This solution, as insulting to men as their consumerist reduction into hip-thrusting animals, will simply be the new and purchasable answer to an older phony problem.

As for children, we are all responsible for creating the conditions of their hazy brains and electronic confusion. Turning a kid into a passive rather than active thinker should be regarded as a crime against humanity.

The typical kid today probably has a completely different understanding of the sensation of boredom from someone born before the rise of digital entertainment. Their summer boredom isn't the kind I experienced. During my childhood, as the locusts droned on outside, time took on the consistency of tree sap turning to amber. Back then, I would build things out of Legos or run around in the pasture or read somebody's romance novels from the back of the cabinet, which gave me a racy *éducation sentimentale*. My grandma even found a way to keep us busy by stringing buttons onto a piece of thread with a needle until it was full, then dumping them and starting all over again. My brother and cousins and I would eat blackberries from the briars, throw soggy plum seeds at each other, collect locust skins in a plastic pail, jump our bikes on dirt hills, or dig with twigs at beds of fire ants. In those summer hours, as hard as I tried, I could not fill them enough to keep the boredom from edging in. But ultimately, that boredom was the necessary precondition for all the best thinking I did.

The boredom of the new kids is a more bothered kind, one that stems from a constant strand of images and sounds unfurled before the eyes and ears. Theirs is sensorial fatigue, whereas mine was sensorial longing. They are never alone without digital custodians. But undisturbed solitude is fundamental for the mind to formulate any thought really worth thinking.

The Russian filmmaker Andrei Tarkovsky once said, "People who grow bored in their own company seem to me in danger." To embrace boredom is to be comfortable alone with oneself. It is unclear why so many people today refuse to be alone. Really, acutely alone. Not in an "I'm spending Saturday night in my bedroom by myself watching YouTube videos" kind of way, but in absolute media-lessness. Free from distractions. You, yourself, and thou. Nothing to mediate your experience of you. Strangely, this kind of self-concentration has the potential to push you outside yourself; you have to quit your own body in order to observe it. Getting out of one's own stubborn subjectivity means not accepting one's role as a passive, porous surface designed solely to absorb the ideas of others. Silence + imagelessness + absence of people + unfilled time = boredom. A recipe for attention.

My dream life is visceral. Every night, sleep is filled with vivid dreams more real than the waking world. These dreams affect my mood for hours after waking and remain crystal clear in my mind, sometimes even years after I dreamed them. They are full of symbols, feelings, physical sensations, figures from my past and present, impossible physics, paradoxes, indescribable colors, repetitions, and animals. They are photo-realistic depictions of things that could never be. I welcome this peek into my subconscious and am thankful that this window is available to me every single night. I know people who never dream; I can't imagine an existence deficient in what I consider absolutely necessary nocturnal fodder for my writing and thinking. These dreams are as much a part of me as my fingerprints. I don't necessarily believe that they're decipherable, that they contain the hidden code of my being or the formula for my psyche. It's just that they are infinitely interesting. For this reason, I often write them down. When I reread these pages, the dream atmosphere returns in one torrent, a full instant download. And I think, "My mind made this," and I feel like a kernel of creative potential.

Dreaming has been described as the mind's way of sorting out all of the input it has received. New and old information is tossed like a salad in the somnolent brain. Details from your day that you may or may not have consciously noticed surface there, bobbing up alongside long-submerged faces and scenes, flotsam and jetsam in the cranial sea.

Then comes the daydream. Is the distinction between dreaming and daydreaming merely whether the eyes are closed or opened? The dream is rarely seen as a form of distracted thinking, since it is an insular phenomenon not in competition with real life. Dreams unfold themselves when the body has nothing to do but lie there. Daydreaming, on the other hand, is the idle man's commerce. It relies on a stepping out of waking life—so-called legitimate life. The daydreamer simply dismisses the prerequisite of sleep. He lets his brain dislodge of its own accord and prompts it on its merry, rising way. The daydream is a living chain of associations; you're wide awake but unencumbered by the strictures of logic or responsibility. It is a nuisance in an efficiency-obsessed system, a curvy line in an ever straighter world.

Have you ever paid attention to the logic of your daydream? What sends you off track? What brings you back? Lately, I've tried retracing my digressive thought chains. When I realize I'm clicking around pages (Internet ones or mental ones), I try to retrace meticulously how I got to a particular site. I pay attention to what caught my eye, what exactly in my psychological composition made me click on that particular link, or what made me click away from a certain page. I turn the whole seemingly dull-minded sequence into an occasion for self-study. After all, the Watchers are recording and studying our digressions online. Shouldn't we have some sense of our own digressive mechanisms?

In the early twentieth century, a serious inquiry into the aesthetic aspects of meandering thought came in the form of stream-of-consciousness literature, with writers such as James Joyce and Virginia Woolf attempting to render the subjective experience of consciousness in words. Up to that point, narrative had gotten quite good at depicting characters from the outside, describing every fold of their clothing and every pore in their skin, cataloging the range of postures and facial expressions, and even probing a little inward and psychologizing the characters and narrators. That is one kind of reality. But the human as perceiving subject was left largely unexplored. What about the world as we perceive it through a subjective filter? What about all the noise, the murmurs and the roars, that the mind brings to any experience? Imagine a character sitting in a room crowded with people. He is able to see them, a few at a time, details of their bodies and their movements popping forth in his consciousness. But his mind also spins out its own ticker tape of memories, judgments, questions, anxieties, and emotions. He is the product of all that has ever befallen him, of all he has thought, of all that he hopes will happen. Trying to capture this in narrative form was the challenge taken up by modernist writers. I find stream-of-consciousness literature difficult to read because my own mind is already kinetic enough; when my thoughts are then superimposed upon an equally chaotic, fictional inner monologue, my brain folds. But I appreciate the effort to show through the medium of literature that we are generally totally unaware of our minds' convulsive nature. The brain swerves and plunges, irrespective of our ignorance of its mechanisms.

In France in the 1960s, an experimental collective of artists, writers, and thinkers named the Situationist International wanted to shake people from their habits and teach them to put trust in intuition and unschooled reflexes. They organized group walks in urban centers like Paris during which they would let the city guide them. The practice was called the *dérive*, or the drift, and was a way to undo the automatism of life in a city. The habit they worked against was that tendency of most urban dwellers to become mechanized in their movements and programmed to repeat the same actions mindlessly. They go to the same three or four spots every day. Their destinations are functionally planned: there is a place whose function is sleeping, another for eating, another for earning money. People forget to notice things while locked in their perfunctory routines. Through the *dérive*, the city would suddenly become visible again—and hearable and smellable—and the participants would walk through it as though Paris were a big, dreaming brain open for digression. They would pay attention to the city's cues, to its natural fissures and pathways and the way it transformed into a completely different city with each passing millisecond, with each new perspective and each new angle of light throughout the afternoon, an inheritance from the Impressionists. From Montparnasse to Porte de la Villette, from Porte Dauphine to Belleville, they made their own bodies into thoughts guided by instinct through parks and alleyways like cognitive threads. The Situationist International believed—and I firmly believe it, too—that it's possible to harness the mind's digressions, its distractions, for the sake of art, self-understanding, science, or pleasure. For example, when you use attention to estrange your familiar patterns—where you walk, what you click, how you order your day, whom you see—the habitual can seem suddenly alien. You are a visitor to your own house. By estranging the familiar, you produce a feeling similar to that of the pilgrim in an unknown land. It is this feeling that has generated some of the most fascinating books, paintings, music, and other cultural experiments in human history. Travel literature is rich because the writer sees clearly what has become invisible to the local. There is no reason such a defamiliarizing of the familiar can't be applied to our own habitat or our own patterns of thinking. It is a matter of constructing a temporary, observational distance between ourselves and our routine thoughts and behaviors. Studying how the brain patches the world together and how it tends to settle in its own dust is a way to put productive questions to one's context and to keep attention from atrophying.

"It is fair to say that there exists in our era a tragic discrepancy between the staggering richness of the visible world and the extreme poverty of our capacity to perceive it." This jewel from Robert Harrison's book *Gardens: An Essay on the Human Condition* draws our awareness to a puzzling conundrum in contemporary America: images, images everywhere and not a thing to see. Pictures crowd us, but this profusion has strangely blunted our perceptual skills. Already in Germany in 1927, Siegfried Kracauer expressed concern about the blinding power of the picture. He wrote, "The blizzard of photographs betrays an indifference toward what the things mean." There is a direct correlation between the abundance of visual material and the inability to decipher critically or to appreciate the aesthetic strength of a particular image. We do not remember how to read images with subtlety. Put another way, each picture *means* less than it ever has before. With their blinding will to self-multiply, images erase the singularity of each one and transform instead into clouds of billowing distraction. By the time the eye gets hold of a picture, another one arrives to displace it. Distraction is caused by too-muchness.

Attention involves the stretching of the self toward something, implicit in the Latin root *tendere* (to stretch), from which the word derives. Attention is a tension, the deliberate tautness of a line of thought between self and object. Once you've attached this line and gotten rid of the slack, you've singled out a unique dyad from an infinite field of possibilities. It is like a constellation: the stars themselves hold no patterns until the human eye traces connections between them. You select an entity and put it in relation to yourself. Or perhaps it is the entity that has selected you.

Attention requires total investment in one thing. To pay attention is to tend to the thing at hand. It is to care for this thing, perhaps to put the self in its place, to think it from all angles and acknowledge all its properties, both mystical and banal. Attention is a form or resistance against the centrifugal pull of our Big Bang universe. Use this metaphor to gather your brain and to invite its cognitive energies to behave in your service. The inside of your head is its own microcosm, mostly composed of dispersed but centralizable matter. Assemble your thoughts on the head of a pin.

The Emotive Spectacle

Feelings are now events. A sample of recent headlines:

- "Pharrell Williams Cries 'Happy' Tears Watching Fan Videos on 'Oprah'"
- "Paris Hilton Angry on 'The View' as She Is Scolded by the Ladies"
- "June Steenkamp Cries During Pistorius Murder Trial"
- "Pelosi Visibly Shaken When '60 Minutes' Confronts Her About Shady Investments"
- "Bode Miller Cries During NBC Interview About His Dead Brother"
- "Visibly Distraught Glen Beck Challenges Black Panthers"
- "Desperate Malaysia Airlines Flight MH370 Families Dragged from Press Room"

- "Robert De Niro Cries on Katie Couric Talk Show"
- "Barack Obama Shows His Anger over AIG Bonus Criticism"
- "LeAnn Rimes Cries on ABC"

In some cultures, emotion is a secret. Anger stays repressed; depression stays taboo; joy stays tempered. Even in times of mourning, sadness is a private matter or strictly a family affair. It is strange to zoom in on suffering faces, or moved ones, or enraged ones, a technique so common in American and European broadcasting. I saw this in Italy on the Miss Italia beauty pageant a few years ago. There, the camera work seemed punitive. As each woman was eliminated from the competition, a close-up shot of smeared mascara and hot tears penalized her for not being beautiful enough. It was uncanny; the camera eye fixated on this pain so much longer than was needed to reinforce the usual narrative of triumph and failure characteristic of pageant culture. The camera eye savored the discrepancy between the model she was and the monster she'd become, an ogress with swollen eyes and convulsing features. The cruel lens sought to prove that this ugliness had been there all along, hidden.

There's some of this on American TV. But there's also a weirder thing going on in the States. There seems to be an emphasis on showing people in the process of feeling strong emotions, which perhaps works in lieu of the audience members' experiencing real emotions themselves. Someone else does all the feeling on your behalf so you can be spared the effort of emoting. Otherwise, why all the insistence on someone's emotional state reported in real time? Why the close-up shots of distress? And the constant harping on how angrily someone expresses herself or how moved someone is by a song? Or maybe it's that the filmed people have to show that they are capable of feeling. Or that cameras automatically trigger erratic emotion. In the worst case, all of this is staged to toy with our mirror neurons. Somebody wants to use empathy against us.

The undeniable fact: emotion has become its own event. Because the media is responsible for filling so much dead time and reading space, they've turned responses to events into events in themselves. Perhaps in the past, AIG bonuses, shady investments, or the Pistorius trial would have been news enough. But now, the emotional response to these events becomes a story in itself. Seeing someone emote publicly is more newsworthy than the boring details of someone slithering through loopholes in the tax code. The face, with its ever-changing muscular countenance, is the new locus of news. Physiognomy is a living ticker. I propose that in addition to specialists like the national security analyst, senior political analyst, and chief business correspondent, a new prestigious position should be created: senior sentiment analyst, whose job it is to close-read the faces and gestures of the famous and the unknown. The idea of emotion as event allows for guilty parties to scuttle away in the dust of the diversion. Smeared mascara bleeds and covers the real problem, like a liquid censor bar.

Intergenerational Conversation

Help the aged. One time, they were just like you: Drinking, smoking cigs, and sniffing glue.

—PULP, "Help the Aged"

I read once that there is a tribe somewhere whose children are completely separated from their parents at birth and are raised instead by their grandparents. The idea is enchanting to me, particularly in relation to my own story. Because my parents had to work a lot, I was raised, along with my brother and cousins, largely by my grandma. I never felt the need to rebel against her, but, starting around age eleven, if not earlier, I constantly revolted against my poor mom. My mother was very close to her own grandmother but had lots of conflicts with her mom (my grandma). I have a lingering fear that someday I'll have a daughter who wants to dress like a princess and who will eventually conform brainlessly to the brainless habits of society, the opposite of what I think is cool. Her kid will be awesome, though. This generational leapfrog will continue ad infinitum. I wonder: if I'd been separated at birth from my mom and raised solely by my grandma, would I have developed the rebellious compulsions that are part of my character? Perhaps I would have lashed out at my grandma nevertheless, but I highly doubt it. There seems to be an eerie compatibility between alternating generations. What is the nature of this synergy?

When they converse, the membrane between generational cohorts is thick. Rarely are we put in a nonhierarchical circumstance of conversation with people outside our own age group. At home, between parents and children, the hierarchy is evident. A similar one exists in the public space. At school, for example, the faculty and administrators are clearly responsible for shepherding the young ones; even the freshman-sophomore-junior-senior class divide is enough to splinter social dealings into age groups. In the workplace, seniority and title play significant roles in the social dynamic. If you are young, the old may seem distant and potentially oppressive, having already gained some form of professional or social legitimacy and not letting you forget their supremacy. They offer unsolicited advice, smile at your naïveté, and instruct you on the countless ways in which the past was better. If you are old, the young seem self-centered, self-destructive, or self-indulgent, absorbed by gadgets and their unearned privilege.

However, I submit that old people and young people are equally cool and more than capable of mutually engaging in conversation.

One of my favorite places to overcome age-based fragmentation is the karaoke bar. If you're lucky, you live in the vicinity of a bar that hosts weekly karaoke and attracts people of all ages and backgrounds. Obviously, you'll meet no people under twenty-one in these bars, but at my favorite karaoke bar in Mountain View, California, it is not unusual to find people over seventy in attendance. Before he passed away, a man named Steve who was in his eighties showed up around nine PM every week and sang "I Did It My Way." He fought in World War Two and told us that his platoon was the first to open the gates of one of the concentration camps. Everyone cheered him heartily when he'd show up, and the nice karaoke DJ Brian would call him up immediately to take the mic. Steve had instant cred because of his age, his kindness, and his pipes. The guy could sing. Music is generally one of the great generational divides between people, but somehow, with a benevolent karaoke audience, people will encourage each other regardless of the song. Those in their twenties cheer on a fifty-year-old lady singing Patsy Cline and the fifty-year-olds cheer on someone in their twenties singing Sir Mix-A-Lot. Karaoke is the great leveler. Having terrible pitch and bad rhythm has rarely kept anyone from grabbing the mic. In fact, sometimes, if you really are terrible, you'll receive a surplus of applause.

There was a regular group of about twenty of us who showed up every week to support one another. The atmosphere in the bar was familial, with lots of nationalities, races, and social classes represented. The old and young sang fantastic duets together. It was always too loud to have a real conversation, but a warm camaraderie was palpable regardless. Let the autumn voices of the old and the springtime voices of the young mix to make new seasons.

The sadness of seniors: it applies to fourth-year high school students, fourth-year college students, and people over sixty-five. All of them suffer from a similar senior melancholy: you are the oldest in a string of generations and you are about to depart for good, never to return. The younger ones look at you with both veneration and scorn. You want to be a freshman again. You have privileges and responsibilities that the others don't have. You know what it's like to belong to the younger cohorts, but they have no idea what it's like to be you. Senioritis is as real for the young as it is for the old.

There is something bittersweet about the moment when you're no longer allowed or you no longer want to sit at the kids' table during holiday dinners. The kids' table, in many ways an infantilizing tradition, keeps the children in their place. This quarantined space invites a kind of youth-based intimacy among cousins who see each other only a few times a year. It is a venue for the exchange of information, prepubescent secrets, jokes, and school-specific culture. In fact, this used to be the primary means of cultural exchange between school districts. I got so many new phrases from a cousin who went to school one district over. (For example, I heard

"Gag me with a spoon" in the '80s for the first time from her; I seem to recall that she improvised her own version: "Gag me with a Smurf." I also remember her singing the tune of "Camptown Races" for my grandfather's birthday, substituting the original lyrics with these: "You're gettin' old and you're gonna die, Doo-da, doo-da.") While we were busy exchanging these arcane middle school confidences, the adults could enjoy some respite and coffee. They could discuss topics in their league: weather, vaguely political themes, and *us*.

The quietest Thanksgiving I ever experienced happened when my grandmother decided to do away with the kids' table and seat us at the table between grown-ups. A similar strategy was used in elementary school by enforcing boy-girl-boy-girl seating. We had a full-size traffic light installed in the lunchroom. When the light was green, we could talk all we wanted. When it was yellow, this was a warning that we were getting too loud. Red imposed total silence. With the boy-girl-boy-girl strategy, the red light was almost never needed. A supreme silence was achieved that Thanksgiving sans kids' table, where the adults did their best to inquire about our schools or hobbies in the greatest detail possible, but the conversation dimmed after the first few minutes. Turkey tryptophan wasn't even needed to lull the discussion. We went comatose together.

I think the problem was simply that we hadn't been trained in intergenerational conversation. When age-based fragmentation is the norm and you get accustomed to communicating only with people your own age, you forget that the old and the young have quite a lot to talk about. To become comfortable with what is unfamiliar: this is the crux of the thing.

Cat Stevens gets me every time with the first verse of "Oh Very Young." It emphasizes life's ephemeral nature and the tendency of childhood dreams to "vanish away like your daddy's best jeans, / Denim Blue, fading up to the sky." These jeans are a metonymy for your dad, who will not last forever despite your most fervent wish that he stay by your side. He will fade up to the sky, like everyone else you love and "the patches make the good-bye harder still." Why must fathers leave us? Can't they just stay?

I remember as a kid I always hated folding my dad's jeans because they were heavy and much longer than my own body, making them difficult to manage. Now, I would happily fold his jeans every single day. I am writing this in a busy café, and a woman in her sixties across the room is smiling at me as she's noticed the tears in my eyes.

Harry Chapin's "Cat's in the Cradle" is another tearjerker. You spend your young life wrapped up in yourself, not yet recognizing what will be missed when it's gone. Tossing the ball around for an hour with your kid becomes a sacred thing when your kid is an adult, too busy with his own family to stop by and say hello. The song morphs a busy young father into a lonely old man, showing how our subjective experience of time changes from one life phase to the next. The priorities of youth keep life's pace quick, too hurried to spend time with others; and in old age, when time congeals, we realize, as the song's narrator does, that the son has grown up just like him, without any time to spare for his father. A friend of mine thinks one of the biggest hidden problems in the U.S. is elderly loneliness. I remember an old episode of *South Park* in which Stan's grandpa locks him in a room and forces him to listen to an Enya-sounding song to illustrate for the boy what it feels like to be trapped in old age. For elderly people without frequent visits from friends and family, time must pass with aching slowness. Loneliness may be our last experience in this world. Solitude can be healthy when it's chosen. When it isn't, it's as heavy as despair. It would be ideal if a steady traffic of companionship would flow throughout one's existence.

The body: a real source of misunderstanding between people of different ages. Imagine that you make it to one hundred years old and you can remember with perfect clarity what it was like to have the body of a one-, ten-, twenty-, thirty-, forty-, fifty-, sixty-, seventy-, eighty-, and ninety-year-old. And imagine that your one-year-old self could have had just as clear a picture of what was to come body-wise up through age one hundred. Walt Whitman was right when he wrote, "I am large, I contain multitudes": each of us is an aggregate of moods, memories, bodily impressions, and genetic heritages. Our bodies are cellular assemblages, which we notice most when they feel either great pleasure or great pain. Think about the sexual nature of your body or what it felt like to run, sleep, or eat at these various ages. The body reveals its lessons gradually through time. This bodily difference limits intergenerational conversation because speech originates in the body; for a conversation to start out on the right foot, the interlocutors have to be sure they have a reciprocal understanding: is the first step of the conversation made by a foot just learning how to walk or by an arthritic one?

The American mall is the necropolis of adolescence. I went to a mall recently and confirmed something strange: the kids who hang out in the mall are the same kids who have always hung out in the mall. They are perfect reincarnations of '80s and '90s children, in all their brashness and conforming non-conformity. They still provoke adults, yell around, flirt with each other, steal things, ride up and down in the elevator, buy candy, and throw food at each other in the food court. They are the ghosts of every teenager who ever loitered in a mall. The impression was uncanny: this stroll through the mall led me past my own past, past the JCPenney, completely untampered with.

An important problem: the vector of advice. Wisdom is transmitted by seepage. It is not unidirectionally dispensed—offered only by the old to the young—but leaks unpredict-ably between ages. What advice might a seven-year-old offer to someone in a midlife crisis? What does a retiree say to someone on their deathbed? What does a thirty-year-old tell someone who's just started her period? Imagine these conver-sations between:

- a young guy who just got dumped by his boyfriend and an old woman whose husband just passed away
- a thirteen-year-old girl and a way older twenty-seven-year-old sister talking about music
- a parent of a three-year-old and a parent of a sixty-year-old

- twin brothers who are thirty and twin brothers who are fifty-five
- someone who is terminally ill at seventeen and someone who is terminally ill at forty-five
- a teen who got her driver's license at eighteen and a man who got his at sixty-two

I love an old headline from *The Onion*: "24-Year-Old Receives Sage Counsel from Venerable 27-Year-Old." Wisdom shared between peers lacks the astute solemnity of advice pronounced by a respectable elder. Still, since we are all so experientially differentiated, each inhabiting a unique body and consciousness, everyone is in a position to offer advice to someone looking for it. I've received sound advice from people of every age.

Young people who kill themselves after being bullied at school may not be able to imagine that life continues long after graduation and that the popular ones who tormented them often had their peak during senior year and went straight downhill afterward. Middle school and high school have a curious way of amplifying themselves to a mammoth scale in the minds of teenagers. Whether you had a positive or a negative experience, you may have been fooled into believing that the real world is simply a macrocosm of school life. But as you move further away from it, it touches you less and proves itself a mere blip in the ever-expanding radar field of your existence. The traumas of school seem negligible now. I don't recall why I was ever angry or distraught or so apt to tip over into despair back in high school. What made me want to sleep all day long and stay up all night on the phone whispering with a friend? We're told that it's just the teen hormone cocktail and the revolting physical metamorphosis that make people this age so volatile. The same thing is said of love: it's merely the outcome of a chemical reaction. My spirit is too poetic to give itself over totally to science. I refuse to believe that any emotion I have is the simple verdict of a chemical process. While it is hard to imagine that I am a living continuation of that alienated person, I cannot dismiss that old despondent self as a chemistry experiment gone sour. What would I say to sixteen-year-old me and what would she say to me? Would she think that I'm cool, happy the way she'd turned out, or would she be disappointed? Would I console her and tell her that things would get better or would I see her as a brat? And as my eighty-year-old self listens in on the conversation in soft bemusement, would she offer advice or just keep quiet?

A universal characteristic of our species is to disparage others. Age discrimination happens every second of every day. One is allowed to insult the old and the young at will— the first, often depicted as grumpy and inflexible and over-conservative ("Creepy old dude!" "You old bag!"), the second as dumb and inexperienced and overliberal ("Spoiled brat!" "Rookie!"). If we were all completely identical—same age, gender, height, weight, race, etc.—we would probably begin to discriminate against each other positionally: "I don't like the diagonal position you're maintaining in relation to mine. Therefore, I hate you." Age discrimination is ugly because it is almost universally permissible. One can always crack old man jokes or dumb teen girl jokes. Even the middle-aged aren't exempt: does the balding guy in a red Ferrari with a girlfriend the same age as his daughter ring a bell? Wait . . . Is there any age that is exempt from mockery? Could age discrimination turn out to be the great unifier since we've all been victims of it?

The word "tween" is as awful a word as "Millennial." I feel sympathy for anyone who has to wear these labels. For whatever reason, "tween" refers almost exclusively to preteen girls, as if there is something so commercially otherworldly about these small ladies, they earned their own marketing demographic. Tweens are cocooned in an in-between phase, no longer children but not yet teens, bearing features of both and displaying very singular needs that distinguish them from the groups around them. There should be words for all of the transitional moments throughout the human life span, not just tweens. The middle-aged person is just as in-between as the tween. Age is the most relative phenomenon. Victor Hugo wrote, "Forty is the old age of youth; fifty the youth of old age."

"Millennial" sounds like a setting on a Casio keyboard that's supposed to imitate the music of a celestial future. The word calls to mind that future scene from *Bill and Ted's Excellent Adventure* when the protagonists' time-traveling phone booth lands them in the ideal civilization they were responsible for creating. Everything is silver and ethereal and only peace seems possible. "Be excellent to each other," is the motto of this future. Yes, the word "Millennial" conveys much-needed hope, but it also smacks of branding. It would be beautiful if a generation could successfully refuse to be named by those who look at it from the outside. The Nameless Ones would spurn the will to baptize. But "Nameless Ones" becomes its own brand as soon as I've typed it.

Walking on Chapel Street in New Haven, Connecticut, across the street from a bus stop where the sidewalk is always full of people, I saw a crowd gathered at the entryway of a small shop that sells jewelry and wigs. There were seven or eight people with concerned faces, bent over something of interest in the doorway. It was a person. As I approached, I saw that it was a black man probably in his late sixties wearing a neon yellow work vest with reflective patches. He was sitting on the cement, slumping against the wall with his hands lifeless at his sides, thick encumbrances. His eyes stared off into space but he saw nothing. His jaw was slack. He must have been working with the men across the street wearing the same reflective vests. He'd had either a stroke or a heart attack. This man was probably someone's dad and grandpa. This big man so broken there on the sidewalk, with people clustered around not knowing what to do, anguished that all they could do was wait for the ambulance to arrive, made me think about my own grandpa who recently passed away. If he had fallen in town, someone would have helped him, too. I'm sure of it. When there is an obvious and pressing need for help, people know how to respond. It is the unsure, slower, protracted need for help that goes ignored. I couldn't stop thinking about this man after I saw him. He felt like a symbol. Did they awaken him from his daze? Did someone lose their grandpa that day? We can't know.

Do you remember the film *Cocoon* from 1985? It was thematically cruel, focused on the impossibility of rejuvenation. We watch elderly people on the screen become young again, if only temporarily, floating in a fountain of youth in the shape of a swimming pool. Eventually, some choose to depart for a distant world without aging or illness. The credits roll and we wake back up to a world without this possibility. An art history teacher of mine in college noted a major difference between the young and the old. Teenagers—especially teenage guys—often fill their notebooks with images of grim reapers and skulls. They sometimes wear black and celebrate morose thoughts about dying. I went to high school with a Goth girl who was rumored to have slept in a coffin. But this fixation stops by itself at a certain age. Have you seen many old people with grim reaper T-shirts? They're close enough to the real thing that they don't have to indulge themselves in fantasies about playing chess with death. They know that the fountain of youth is a wishful illusion. Florida is as close as you can get.

A little man, no younger than ninety-five, with a cap on his head, hobbled in with his cane and sat next to me at a café. "Those are interesting shoes," he said of my black leather boots. "Thank you." He sat a while and read his paper, drinking a cup of tea. On his way out, he said, "If I were a little younger, I'd flirt with you." Then he walked out. When you're old, you can say what you want. This is the great privilege of the autumn years: true freedom of speech.

There is a specific place where elderly people can look for love: the personals section of the *New York Review of Books*. When the new issue arrives each month, this is the first place I turn, not because I'm looking for an "athletic widower," but because these pages reveal the tirelessness of human hope. The yesteryear vocabulary is the first clue that the people writing these ads are old folks: feisty, slender, affluent, slim, and "easy on the eyes" confirm we are not scrolling through twentysomething OKCupid profiles. One of my favorites simply reads: "Dear Santa, Please put one lovely man in his sixties under my tree." In the self-descriptions, women often portray themselves as fit, intelligent, passionate, sophisticated, and exotic; one woman described herself as "satin mocha complexioned." Men often specify they're looking for someone petite and tender, words that imply that their intimate histories have been populated by mean lady giants. Or perhaps it is a nice way for the gentleman to be clear he's seeking a sweet woman who isn't too chubby. The words "vibrant" and "active" are used frequently, reinforcing the fact that old age doesn't have to mean decrepitude. The vital force asserts itself in these ads, each one declaring categorically: "I refuse to die." The authors paint enchanting scenes of the kinds of evenings and afternoons to come should a successful match happen: wine tasting weekends in Napa, slow walks through Paris, trips to the theater, and even treks through the Amazon. These are pictures straight out of commercials, collective rather than personal dreams. A sadness lingers in some of the solicitations written by people who recently lost their longtime spouses. I even came across one ad in which the man writes that his wife is "fading away"—perhaps from Alzheimer's or another slow disease—and that he is looking for companionship. It seems callous to start looking for someone new even before the bed has cooled, but I imagine that losing a wife of fifty years very slowly is the kind of experience that, more than any other, requires someone at your side in order for you to endure it. Another man writes that he is in a very unhappy marriage and looking for a lady friend who might be in the same situation. It is remarkable to think of all the people who are utterly alone in their relationships and who endure it for decades. Alone together, a configuration suited for our times. I am most fond of the kick-ass old ladies who describe themselves as klutzes on the dance floor but who love to dance anyway. They seem much more full of verve than I am and eager to provoke life, the way a matador would. What is it that just hatches in some people at age seventy, transforming them into joyful acrobats? How does the epiphany stir, prodding you to remember that life happens just once?

August 16, 2001: the day I found my first grey hair. I know this because I still have it, labeled, dated, and taped in a huge notebook I keep full of drawings and thoughts and poems. I was twenty-three years old then. Terribly proud, I wanted to keep it as a symbol of my progress toward financial independence, freedom of speech, flourishing wisdom, and the liberty to circulate wherever I wanted to go in the world. Most of the cool people in my life had tons of silver on their heads and in their eyebrows. Because I'd been lucky to spend so much time with my awesome grandma as a kid, I had a very positive impression of seniors. When I got my first job at sixteen, my favorite coworker was a woman named Linda who was old enough to be my grandmother. Ever since, I've always spent as much time as I could with people over fifty.

I was never that fond of people my own age or younger, but things have shifted in my mind over the past few years. As a professor, I spend a lot of my time around people between eighteen and twenty-five or so. This is completely stimulating. I don't remember being interesting at that age, but these students are mesmerizing in the breadth and depth of what they do. Especially in my office or over coffee, away from the classroom, they reveal so much about what it's like to be young in a world that's gotten weird and aggressive. They are small and highly polished professionals, without much time or room or encouragement to think or wander aimlessly. They are as tenderhearted as twenty-year-olds ever were, but the impulse toward romanticism is kept in check by pragmatism. Their habits haven't yet petrified, and this malleability, they are told, will be good for their careers. I ask them a lot of questions about music, about cultural currents kept hidden from the grown-ups; I ask how it feels to be starting or finishing their studies and what they're thinking about in general. A simple, open-ended question and they let loose with everything. They are generous and humble and vulnerable and very wise about things I was unwise about. But their singularity has been groomed out of them. They are so much more observed and hovered over than I was; their speech patterns are identical; they show little resistance to conformity. The media depicts sexting and hookups as scandalous acts, but read Joan Didion's essay "Slouching Towards Bethlehem" to see what twentysomethings in San Francisco were doing in 1967 and you'll reconsider what counts as scandalous. (It abounds with free love and not-so-free love, and in one episode, a five-year-old is given peyote.) Kids' lives today are extremely tidy. Their parents reconnoiter them at home, and their friends do it wherever else they may be. Social surveillance puts them in a situation of forced levity and perpetual fun having, but I get the impression that the strange tug-of-war they live between professional seriousness and mandatory frivolity produces nothing but anxiety in them. There is no space apart for them to just *be*. Nowhere is neutral. Their parents are much more present in their daily lives than mine were when I was in college, even though most of them are much farther from home. They still have some kind of contact with everyone in high school and everyone they ever met, even those they never cared that much about. Their cross-country move to this isolated campus wasn't a sharp break; they can still know what their best friend from elementary school ate for dinner that night. Their old life has only bled into the new one. No rupture, no initiation, no absolute fracture from the past. Temporally and spatially, everything is present. Furthermore, they are urged to turn banalities into events, hyperconscious that each photo they take will become a memory. They are afraid of loss because they've been told how horrible it is by older people. The now has to be *celebrated* every second, to the detriment of actual experience. I don't know if I could live how they've been asked to live, but maybe everyone thinks that about the generation behind them. I feel too slow and too melancholic and too unprofessional to live that way. I care about those details of life that they document at every second with words or pictures, but I don't want a camera or a keyboard to intervene between me and those details as I meet them. I like to spend a lot of time outside the social world. There's probably something addictive about living suspended between the pull of high-energy professionalism and the pull of unremitting entertainment. But I want to stay a bored amateur.

Recently, I got a glimpse of a very different kind of adventurous youth far, far removed from my students. At the 2014 exhibition "Italian Futurism, 1909–1944: Reconstructing the Universe," visitors to the Guggenheim Museum in New York saw a veritable fetishism of youth and aggression. The Futurist project centered on the heroism of war and the conflation of the youthful male body with the sleek machine. This vision of youth stands in stark contrast to the contemporary American one where, despite the celebration of youthful violence through video games and other media, the young person's survival is more coveted than ever. Those young Italians back in the early twentieth century made art that sang the praises of speed and war, "the world's only hygiene." The Futurists were by no means bearers of a mainstream message, but it is difficult to imagine an equivalent in contemporary America. Even today's gun enthusiasts are traditionalists; they invoke the wishes of the Founding Fathers relentlessly and look toward history for clues about how to live. On the contrary, the Futurists wanted to tear down tradition, demolish museums, put a torch to history, and start from scratch in a new age of steel. Theirs was not just empty talk; many of them volunteered and died in World War One. I cannot imagine a group of young artists now crafting a violence-centered aesthetic that they would actually die for. The Futurists were intellectuals, many from very cultured backgrounds. This is true of many of my students as well. But who among them would paint a canvas with the image of a fighter jet and then die in the flames of one as it crashed? This comparison I make—an intentionally jolting one—helps show the great variety of forms a philosophy of youth can take, limited only to the West and to a span of one hundred years.

When I stood in front of Boccioni's sculptures, Carrà's paintings, and Marinetti's words-in-freedom poetry, my thoughts strangely went to their parents. What must it have felt like to have a child who would happily have died in a flaming car crash? A contemporary twenty-year-old expressing any Futurist inclinations would probably be sent immediately to a counselor at the university clinic. An intervention staged by family and friends would remind the misguided youth that life is a gift and that its preservation is the only objective of civilization. A Futurist is unimaginable in contemporary America. There is no equivalent. Youth here and now does not crave danger. It craves simulations of danger.

Our perceptions of size change with age. Thoreau wrote a beautiful sentence about the shifting size of ambition throughout a life: "The youth gets together his materials to build a bridge to the moon, or, perchance, a palace or temple on the earth, and, at length, the middle-aged man concludes to build a woodshed with them." To age is to move from the conditional to the indicative. Youth is composed of more questions than answers; old age boasts an equal amount of each. I have a strange fantasy: I wish there were giant people in whose laps I could sit. I don't want to be a child again; I just wish that there was a giant person who would read to me for hours as I nestled in her warmth.

Is it strange that I'm eager to be old? That I find elderly people so astonishingly significant, the most prized thing we have? I don't know how we forgot this. I recently watched a Canadian documentary called *When Jews Were Funny* (2013) whose director, Alan Zweig, interviews Jewish comedians of all ages and expresses his sentimentality over the humor, mannerisms, and spirit of the elderly people who'd surrounded him when he was growing up but who have mostly passed away. In the last scene, the director asks Shelley Berman, a comedian in his late eighties who played Larry's father on *Curb Your Enthusiasm*, whether his children will grow to be old Jews in the way that he did. Berman says that his daughter will certainly not be an old Jew, that she's hardly a modern-day Jew, and that he lost his son before he turned thirteen years old. After expressing the difficulty of this loss, he begins spontaneously to sing an old song in Yiddish. He finishes the verse but doesn't stop. He keeps going. He keeps on singing. The comedian doesn't get a laugh from me; he gets me weeping. There I am again, crying about a beautiful oldness that will be irretrievable very soon, the song itself inspired by loss. Our old folks are receding waves. They know things that they'll take with them when they go. Just talk to them. They're from an age when people did that still. It will be even more of a gift to yourself than to them.

Toward a Sterile Future

The ubiquity of antibacterial hand-sanitizing dispensers that now populate the public space should be a reminder that the war on filth has been institutionalized. If it's not terrorists who threaten the cleanliness and godliness of our pristine nation, it's the militant microbes who seek to undermine our (hygienic) constitution. We elect a cleaner future.

As with everything else, there are clear consumerist motivations behind this sanitary craze. It doesn't cost anything to smell like oneself. Of course, it is more profitable to sell people products that help them get clean than to let them sit with contentment in their own natural grime. This goes far beyond the mere hygienic necessities that prevent the spread of disease. The slightest hint of BO is enough to make many Americans scrunch their noses in disgust, as if their own pits naturally bore the crisp scent of lilacs in a dewy April field. (Already the fact that there is a fixed set of initials for "body odor," which everyone knows, indicates a general complicity in the phobia; BO, the BM, and the BJ make clear that people require initials to make their grossness abstract.) Here, we're dealing with politicized hygiene, class tensions, and control: he or she who smells bad is demoted on the social hierarchy. The smell of someone else's body is perceived as a violation, an unsolicited nasal penetration. Such an olfactory affront can be met only with disdain, or, worse, hostility. My character is judged by my scent trail. But the smell of someone's unmasked skin is as authentic and honest as a fingerprint; it cannot be counterfeit.

Can you imagine an alternate universe in which dirtiness is the ideal? People line up to buy sacks of manure, mud baths replace perfume counters, and eau de cologne is swapped for eau de colon. Miss Piggy would abandon her mascara and return to the sty. The overripe smell of perspiration and reality would replace the pungent sting of bleach and Febreze. The great unwashed would govern the fragrance junkies.

The current antiseptic attitude undoubtedly changes the way one dwells in the world. It weakens our literal and figurative immune systems and exemplifies our dread of risk. Dirt and germs crop up and spread in an unforeseeable fashion, disrupting itineraries and complicating what should be simple. To avert this unpredictability, one douses every surface with disinfectant and fumigates with fabric mists and sanitizing sprays and air fresheners, just like medieval Europeans who believed they could stave off the plague and cover its insistent stench by smothering their noses in sweet-smelling flowers. The latest "scent technology" devices warm up in the socket and distribute the smell around the house; some even have little fans to facilitate the spread of the holy linen-scented incense in domestic and professional spaces. Will the smell of Fresh Rain™ replace the smell of fresh rain?

The killing of germs is the literal version of our antiseptic drive, but there are also symbolic iterations. Clean surfaces are appealing, but so are clean lines. The contours of our computers should be as smooth as the contoured eyebrows of the television news anchor. The knowing curve of her penciled brow conveys precision and perfectionism. She is well groomed, which must mean that she is a reliable source of information. Based on image alone, one imagines her emitting Chanel fragrance from every pore, as though her glands had been replaced by delicate crystal bottles of the stuff. Her coanchor is no less groomed and fragrant, the perfect equilibrium of grey and grace, a real thoroughbred of the Just for Men variety. They are scripted people, suckling their life essence from the teleprompter. No room for unpredictability or contingency. Away with wrinkles, cellulite, stray hairs, a turncoat strand of lint, curvy deviations, or any other disruption of the sacred straightness.

As people become increasingly digital beings, one finds in the world of computers and telephony evidence of an attraction to a clean aesthetic and risk-free technological engagement. In the '90s, during the heyday of the PC, there was a certain dirtiness (grunge) and recklessness (extreme sports) that have now been replaced by the sterile cleanness of Apple products and the risk-averse habits of digital living. Messiness and danger are no longer desirable. The extreme sports of the 1990s—skydiving, bungee jumping, the X Games— have been supplanted by navel-gazing activities like social networking and video gaming, free of bodily danger and without a real investment of the corporeal self. Now, it is possible to break up with someone via text message without ever needing to explain things face-to-face. Peril and discomfort are successfully averted.

There is something uncanny about the sanitary aesthetic of Apple products, which construct a world free of germs and risks. They take for granted a populace that sees no value in the character-building virtues of things not easily had. There was a time when the PC and the Mac were starkly different brands. Their aesthetic and functional differences have decreased over time, but the stereotypes about them and their target markets have lingered. The residual rivalry between devotees of the PC and of the Mac includes within it dozens of points of access for a critique of American culture. The fact that this debate exists and that the two camps are so clearly defined illustrates the extent to which we sometimes think in unambivalent terms and work through our heavier collective, psychosocial problems in the form of petty arguments over something as insignificant as brand preference. It resembles the scenario in which you see a couple fighting ruthlessly about the laundry or the checking account; these are often mere surface pretexts to discuss unseen, momentous things. You know their argument has nothing to do with the dirty towels but involves the very fabric of the relationship.

What is really at stake in the residual debate between the Mac and the PC is whether it is preferable for technology to insinuate itself seamlessly into existence or to remain compartmentalized and external to our personhood. Also at stake is whether a loss of the need—and ability—to deal with ugliness and unpredictability is an emancipation or an imprisonment. I see the old debate between the Mac and the PC as a metaphor for two kinds of possible futures, both of which give reason for pause. Two choices are offered, a one or a zero, as if choice were digital rather than analog.

One's worldview can be partially deduced based solely on a preference for the PC or the Mac. I guess I should reveal in which camp I find myself. I own a Macbook Pro, an iPad mini (a gift), and an iPod (also a gift). I have an iMac at the university, which I requested to replace the PC used by the previous occupant of the office. I didn't own a Mac until around 2009, when I was converted by a Mac apostle who believes fervently in the superiority of Apple products. Upon my conversion, I felt a light enter my heart. I suddenly had a clear vision of what was possible through digital technology. I was purged of my fear of viruses. The virtues of quick processing and un-buggy computing were revealed to me. But I am no Mac zealot. I will explain why.

I had resisted buying a Mac because I was put off by the self-righteous way Apple advocates make their opinions known. In general, self-convinced congregations are very unappealing to me. So I resisted. But I had my own justifications. The Mac and its accoutrements all seemed like unnecessary eye candy, a way to keep people buying new things they don't need and to feed their consumerist cravings. Planned obsolescence, pure and simple. For me, it was also a class question. Something about Mac culture struck me as elitist and exclusive. So I clung to my PC. It had no frills. It was unwieldy and clumsy, but it could more or less carry out the modest tasks I requested of it. I was a student and didn't have loads of disposable cash lying around, so I didn't see the point in spending a significant amount of money just so I could buy the kind of laptop all my classmates had. But after the hard drive on my PC died a couple of times and I recognized the uselessness of my investments to resuscitate it, I thought it was time to make a change.

I still have occasional contact with PCs. Many university libraries both in the U.S. and in Europe still have them, so when I don't feel like pulling out my Mac, I resort to the on-site computers to look up books or find references. Granted, the universities would probably all switch to Macs if they had the means, but they are bound to these old machines for financial reasons. It would be hard to convince the administration to replace all of them since they still more or less get the job done, even if they are cosmetically inferior. What's more, they lend a certain nostalgic air to any library, somehow complementing the dusty tomes and the obsolete card catalogs that wait to no avail in the corners for someone to use them. I enjoy coming across a friendly old PC who greets me in its own cumbersome, folksy fashion, like Wilford Brimley. Revisiting these familiar friends from my own days as an undergrad, I find comfort in their bulk. The buttons are thick and resemble typewriter keys more than the relatively soundless and compact Mac buttons. The old PC keys jut out of the keyboard surface unnecessarily; one could imagine popping them out one by one like grey, plastic teeth from unwell gums. The Mac keys, on the other hand, seem inseparable from the surface in which they are embedded. They feel smart and clean, as if the people who designed them really had it together. Almost *too* together.

The perceived symbolic differences between the two brands have been rehearsed in many contexts. The most famous is perhaps the 2006 Mac ad campaign that gives an anthropomorphic form to each brand. John Hodgman plays the role of PC. He is a nerd, a business type. He is awkward and unattractive, and thinks in terms of spreadsheets and other corporate necessities. The Mac role is played by Justin Long, a young guy, cool and unassuming, who purports to be more interested in life than in business. The viewing audience probably ultimately preferred Hodgman's character, the laughable embodiment of the stiff PC, because he provides comic relief, but in the end, it doesn't really matter whom you prefer. The ad is rigged so that whichever character you favor, you'll still side with Mac because it is Apple who has framed the argument and articulated the (imagined) difference between the two brands in clear and digestible terms. Finally, you clearly see the distinctions between Mac culture and PC culture. If you are young, cool, and globally and digitally savvy, you will naturally gravitate toward the Mac. If you are an older, whiter, business-oriented person (often male) or in some way allied with this demographic; if you are really into gaming; or if you know nothing about computers, you will go for the PC. And because the PC can never be dissociated from the world of Big Corp and all the cultural baggage embodied—very often unfairly—in the figure of the older white male, it is clear that the Mac is the only viable choice for people who have their eye on the future. The distinction is laid before us in such a clear-cut fashion, we don't even have to think about it critically anymore.

(A footnote in Jonathan Franzen's *The Kraus Project* expresses similar hesitations about Apple. Franzen has a problem with Apple's coolness and opts instead for the sobering uncoolness of the PC. I particularly like this observation he makes: "I could easily imagine the PC being played by a German actor and the Mac by a Frenchman, never the other way around." I must admit that I'm sympathetic to Franzen's

Germanophilia and his love of what is heavy and serious. Seriousness, after all, is the secret motivation of everything written here, regardless of what the surface says.)

Most students I've had since I became a professor in 2011 own Macs, particularly the undergrads. When I go to a coffee shop in a big city—especially on the East Coast, on the West Coast, or in Europe—most people have Macs. But when I go home to Texas and sit in public places with Wi-Fi, I see many more PCs. The consistency of this observation frustrates me; I prefer messier realities. It seems that our inflexible socialization determines every single consumer choice we make.

First, it is important to point out that it isn't necessarily your own, personal agency enacting the decision to choose one brand over another; it is often the product that selects you. Imagine if Apple and the PC manufacturers traded target markets: the Mac advertising would suddenly aim to attract corporate America and the PC ads would gear themselves toward a younger, more creative, and aesthetically oriented crowd. This actually makes a lot of sense. The business folks would be happy with their investment in efficient, virus-free machines and the hip young ones could tout their awkward, vintage PC hardware as fetish objects with the same kind of appeal as hipster couture. When one opts for a Mac or a PC, one is playing a highly personalized hand. Your product is an extension of yourself, telling something about you in the same way that wearing a Mohawk or a head scarf does. You show a visible signature of your affiliation—a political, religious, or philosophical one—by choosing this accessory or that one. And the laptop and other portable devices are readable signs in the public space, whether or not they're meant to be.

For this reason, the cosmetic design of the apparatus is of crucial importance. It sends an immediate signal that leads to conclusions about you. In the moment of this interpretive reflex, it is irrelevant whether the conclusions drawn are accurate. Apple understands this very well. "But wait," the PC advocate interjects, "isn't Apple just interested in the surface? Aren't they just fancy designers who are good at making things look pretty?" A dissenter could argue that the Mac both looks better *and* performs better. (Again, I emphasize that the brands resemble each other more and more, so these differences are now probably more imagined than real.) They didn't just design the material aspects of the Mac; they designed the user experience. The Apple designers think like Bauhaus designers. Rather than accepting the well-established givens of the relationships between the form of objects and their function, the Apple-Bauhaus-Collective (ABC) tries to undo assumptions about how something can be put together. For example, I remember when Apple made a very big deal about how it had figured out that a laptop could be much lighter if its body was crafted from a single piece of aluminum. I can't help but see a parallel in Marcel Breuer's Wassily chair, designed in the Bauhaus workshop in 1925–1926. Like the Apple folks, Breuer undoubtedly asked himself, "Why must a chair be made of four legs, a seat, and a backrest? Is there a different way to fulfill this function while putting the object together in another configuration?"

We are still largely dependent on design analogies. The keyboard must be like typewriter keys; the screen must be like a television. But humans didn't learn to fly until they abandoned the analogy of the flying machine as bird. The plane that flapped its wings never got far. But when people adopted a different analogy—the geometrical plane—or maybe functioned independently of conscious analogy, the airplane came to be. Rollable keyboards and Google Glasses start to do away with some old technological analogies, and there will undoubtedly be even more significant shifts in analogical design in the future. And speaking of the future, this is exactly what Apple products are designed to resemble. By imagining what the future could look like and approximating its form, we precipitate the future and make it arrive prematurely. People are impatient to know how it will all turn out, so they project what tomorrow might look like onto the material of today. Voilà. The future is now for sale.

Up until the point when PC manufacturers felt compelled to start imitating the Apple aesthetic, there were two semi-options: the clean lines of the Mac or the boxy lines of the PC. Apple products in general want to smooth over all of the roughness of life. The sterile contours of these objects give the illusion that existence is seamless and clean. They want to braid all aspects of a person (vocation, leisure, thought) into one glassy strand.

I took a course once with the French philosopher Michel Serres, who argued that the reason the Belgian comic book character Tintin has such a wide appeal is that the simple, clean traits of his face allow readers to project themselves onto the character. The blank and generic surface of Tintin's face serves as a tabula rasa for self-inscription. A similar argument can be made about Apple products. They strive for a kind of blankness you can personalize. They are neutral and ready for appropriation. They create a utopian vision, utopian in the etymological sense: that which has no place. Spotlessness. They aim to set up shop in an undetectable non-place, a factory of the impalpable. Whereas Apple's design objective was once to be seen (recall the garish colors of the iMac G3?), in the future—which is to say, the now—these products are threaded into our lives to the point that they go nearly unnoticed. Apple creates the silky illusion that life can be managed; it wants to erase all of your cares and make you indebted to it for having saved you so much time and energy. It wants to glide without a sound into your routine, like an electric eel. This is Apple's ultimate objective: to be invisible.

In its earlier iterations, the PC asserted itself in one's field of vision like a boulder. It was in your face, a loud and plastic fact. Real life resembles the PC and Microsoft software more than the Mac. Real life is illogical, clunky, prone to glitches, and susceptible to viruses. Real life frustrates one's intuitions. Working on a PC teaches you about patience, how to deal with adversity, how to face unpredictability, and how to expect the worst. I can't help but associate the PC with the military-industrial complex; its dark, dense material is reminiscent of heavy artillery. As much as the military-industrial complex would like to be efficient, stealthy, and imperceptible, it tends toward quagmire confusions and unmanageable messes. It gets infiltrated. It leaks. Secrets spill out across its concrete floors. A contemporary Italian writer I'm very fond of named Claudio Magris made a nice wordplay with the PC, likening it to the Communist Party, which is PC in Italian (*Partito comunista*). This pun works in French (*Parti communiste*) and in Spanish and Portuguese as well (*Partido comunista*). In one fell swoop, the PC (Personal computer or *Partito comunista*) can edit history, erasing public memory, selectively deleting unpleasant events. Magris takes his wordplay further by likening Siberia and Cyberia, the cold, digital wasteland where the political prisoner is forced to carry out his sentence after having violated the hidden ethics of international cyberpolitics. That Edward Snowden has ended up in Russia is a fortuitous extension of this metaphor.

Machines and applications today want to address all needs by category and to smooth the distinctions between these categories: the sentimental (photo editing, archiving of memories), the domestic (home security, entertainment), the communicative (phone, e-mail, all non-face-to-face contact with other humans), the bureaucratic (office tasks), the financial (managing your money online), the consumer (buying stuff), the gastronomic (Siri telling you where to eat), the intimate (sex tips, Skype hotness, pornography), the orientational (GPS tracking your every move, helping you get your bearings), the creative (making music, writing stuff, editing videos), the medical (info about your body and future biotech stuff that even your phone will be able to do), and countless other categories. These spheres are still compartmentalized to a certain extent, but the ultimate objective is to remove the boundaries that divide private life from public life, business from leisure, and home from elsewhere. Eventually, everything will be arranged so that you have to take *all* technology or none of it. In other words, if you want to use even the most basic technological features, you will have to plug in *all the way.* Sartre's protagonist in *Nausea* says that if you exist, you have to exist all the way. There is no half-measure order of existence. The same will be true of virtual life: half-plugging will not be possible.

You recognize by now that I am exaggerating the differences between the Mac and the PC to raise questions about how we will proceed in our digital future. In reality, there are fewer and fewer differences between the brands. We feel lucky to have two choices, though I'm not sure we actually have much of a choice at all. It's like our two-party political system in the U.S. in which anyone who is not a Democrat or a Republican has virtually no shot at a share of power. To complicate matters, voters are instantly stuck when their position on the issues doesn't follow party lines. For example, if a voter is fiscally conservative but socially progressive, how does he vote? How does an evangelical who believes in ecologically conscious governance vote? How should someone vote who was horrified by Newtown and believes a serious reassessment of our gun policies is in order but who is opposed to gay marriage? To compound this fact, the parties often resemble each other once they get elected into office anyway. I think we're all more or less aware that the size of our government does not shrink during Republican presidencies, and that there are not fewer armed conflicts or less surveillance, during Democratic ones. It's rather like the same song in a slightly different key, a tom*ay*to or a tom*ah*to. Binary difference ultimately translates into sameness. Because of the petrified nature of our political system, we will likely never see a proliferation of interstitial parties. There will probably never be a viable Green Tea Party, even though the term has been tossed around (mostly as a pun); still, it is worth imagining, as a thought experiment, what such a party might be like. Alas, the elephant-donkey hybrid is probably destined to remain in the realm of the hypothetical. For those of us who have spent time in countries with many viable political parties, the return to the U.S. system feels like frequenting a supermarket with two kinds of food: bread or potatoes. Or a store with two kinds of computers: PC or Mac. My point is that when a dichotomy presents itself as a clean decision between two clearly defined ideas, it is perhaps wise to suspend one's final judgment and to dwell longer on the fact of a system that presents life in such unambiguous terms. Sometimes, what seems to be the most obvious choice is rather the veneer for a murkier reality.

There is a peculiar place we can look to find an example of life before the Apple sterility I've described: Richard Linklater's 1991 cult film *Slacker*, a plotless movie that volleys from weirdo to weirdo in an aimless and uncanny ricochet. Back in the '90s when I first saw it, I found it boring because the characters and setting too closely resembled my own daily life. I could just take a walk down Fry Street near my college campus and see the same folks or, better yet, wait for the weekend and the kooks would show up on my doorstep. I recently re-watched it and was moved nearly to tears by a stark realization that the kind of earthy, imperfect, digressive, and messy humanity depicted in the film is all but extinct among today's middle class. The people portrayed in the movie were certainly never representative of the mainstream; on the contrary, they typified the bohemian underbelly of (sub)urban America. But, while they were considered social outcasts by many in their day, they provided an alternative to the starched and dry-cleaned narratives about what life should look like. People who belonged to this now nearly extinct type, those who were openly critical of consumerist culture and certain social injustices, don't seem to have gone further underground; they seem to have been fumigated. You might still see a scruffy-faced, tattooed man around the neighborhood, but he will almost invariably have an iPhone in his hand.

The film is set in Austin, the weirdness capital of Texas. I didn't go to college in Austin but in Denton, Texas, which could be considered in many ways the Austin of the Dallas–Fort Worth metroplex. Denton was a weird place in the '90s. I lived in a neighborhood known as Cement City, a pretty run-down area with lots of cheap apartments, abundant amounts of drugs, and many strange goings-on. I was surrounded by artists and musicians, unemployed or ambiguously employed people who were no longer students (or who never had been), and strange characters like Bad Dog, a guy who would catch squirrels on campus and stuff their corpses with clay, or the frighteningly gaunt woman with dyed-black hair who claimed that aliens had implanted a glass rod in her body. Human curiosities regularly showed up at our apartment: Iggy Pop look-alikes, pale-faced Goths, strung-out performance artists, and even a British dominatrix.

I didn't care for *Slacker* back then, but why does it move me now? I can only partly attribute my wistfulness to nostalgia. It's true, those were interesting times (I wouldn't call them *good*, but I would call them interesting and, at times, even fascinating from an anthropological point of view), but I generally keep my postadolescent sentimentality tightly corked. The '90s were not all frolicking and plaid flannel. But something has changed fundamentally about middle-class life. The middle class is smaller now, which could explain in part the relative absence of these characters today. What is more disturbing is that the middle class has become very standardized, with a much smaller range of how one can *be*. I seem to recall walking in random cities back in the '90s and seeing a great variety of types. In the large urban centers, this is mostly still true, with a lot of variation from neighborhood to neighborhood. But there seems to be a much clearer standard now of what to wear, how to talk, and what kind of places to frequent. Because we've opted collectively for a chain culture, this means that the same restaurants, clothing stores, coffee shops, and even national news channels are uniformly available from region to region. Whether you visit Chicago, Charlotte, or Cheyenne, you're going to find a Starbucks that makes you forget which zip code you're in. Once this pattern is in place, uniformization is easy. There is comfort in the fact that your drink of choice can be had across the globe ("tall skinny caramel macchiato, *s'il vous plaît*"), with the same kind of stir stick, the same handpicked tunes whose coolness is infectious, and the same beaconlike logo saving you from the unbearable newness of an unknown city.

What moves me about *Slacker* is that Starbucks does not make an appearance in it. The people look at one another and talk to one another. Their conversations may be strange— and probably annoying to those who favor logocentrism and efficiency—but they are at least engaged in face-to-face interaction. They think hypothetically and digressively and have no plan for their lives. Instead, their existence is one prolonged improvisation. And to me, these crooked and erratic lines of a spontaneous existence are poignant and altogether too rare in a culture that must have a plan in order to feel protected from the future. Instead, these characters recognize the creative potential of uncertainty.

The first thing the film made me notice is the tendency today to live fearfully. The current aversion to risk and danger in any form is made blatant through a comparison of the current moment to that little slice of time and space: Austin in the '90s. Yes, it is a fiction film. But the actors portray a life-style that hasn't the slightest tinge of defensiveness to it. One has the impression that people then were vastly less afraid. The film is certainly populated with conspiracy theorists who obsess about everything from the Kennedy assassination to Elvis sightings, outlandish theories about NASA, the green-house effect, missing children, and a hidden alien spacecraft on the moon. But somehow, this doesn't keep them from moving with unfettered spontaneity through their shabby world. They have their suspicions about the government, about collaborations between the U.S. and the Soviet Union, and about political manipulation, but that doesn't keep them from talking to random strangers and going somewhere with-out knowing exactly what will happen to them when they arrive there. They seem wholly unbothered by danger they might encounter in daily life. In comparison to today, the era of overreaction and jittery trigger fingers, the people of *Slacker* tend to *underreact* to scenes of danger (a hit-and-run accident, an arrest, a home robbery). An incident of a man shooting a gun on the highway is described by one character as "beautiful." Kids break sodas out of a vending machine and run unaccompanied through piles of rubble with rusty metal and concrete everywhere. People take random rides from strangers or go to hear a band with someone they don't know at all. All the noise about hookup culture and drunken stupors has made it seem that today's youth is interested in taking all kinds of risks, but I have the distinct impression that this is almost purely a media construction. One could cite all sorts of recent statistics that prove the rampancy of young recklessness, but remember that this recklessness unfolds within the confines of the buffered and sterile societal frame I've described. If you're in trouble, you have a cell phone. There are surveillance cameras everywhere. It is likely you have helicopter parents hovering over you. (I'm still talking about the middle class here.) You're sensitive enough to creepiness that it is very unlikely you will go somewhere with someone you don't know at all. You've been conditioned to fear others. There are many more barriers in place to keep you safe—from others and from yourself—than there were twenty years ago. The paradox is that life is in many ways supposedly safer than it was, but we're that much more fearful for our safety. An interesting theory: that security actually breeds fear.

This brings us to the second notable characteristic of these anti-characters: their improvisational genius. They seem to have no constraints on their schedules, no restrictions imposed by their entourage, no limitations on what is possible in an evening. They ricochet, like the camera itself, from situation to situation, without a clear sense of intention or a final destination. Definitive choice remains in a state of suspension. They let the moment and its circumstances act upon them as it will. They have not been initiated into the cult of the busy. The charm of the film resides in the jazz-like riffs of speech the characters emit as they engage with friends, acquaintances, or total strangers. The first scene shows a young guy improvising a theory of alternate universes to the cabdriver who takes him from the bus station into town. A café philosopher spews out aphorisms (this role is played by Linklater himself). Another guy theorizes about politics as his friends play a game of hand slap. The characters' home addresses are uncertain; they move around at will, untraceable in a presurveillance state, unreachable on the phone or via e-mail. One guy asks another, "Where you headed?" to which he replies, "Oh, I've got some band practice in about five hours, so I figured I'd mosey on out." All in all, their world follows the logic of a Surrealist digression in which time is meaningless, the trip trumps the destination, and people roam without obligations, a calendar, or a watch. Today, it takes a concerted effort *not* to know what time it is. The average middle-class person has to think carefully about how to organize time in real life. However, online life follows a different set of rules. While many hours of aimless digression are voluntarily donated to the Internet, few people now would commit such time to real-life digressions. Why is the only acceptable form of digression today a digital one? The dawdlers and dreamers who reside outside the screen are considered losers and time wasters. But somehow, the online version of this aimlessness is possibly the most frequent pastime in American life. The dawdlers of *Slacker* make life itself into a browsable network.

The third fascinating contrast between the *Slacker* world and our contemporary one is the treatment of money and material culture. If Linklater were to return to Austin today, camera in hand, he might still find some weirdos in the same old coffee shops, but most of them (especially the ones of the same age as the *Slacker* characters) would probably be staring at a screen. Is it possible to be original with these blinking boxes before our eyes? The '90s anti-characters cannot rely on devices or material wealth—they have none—to organize their lives. What would they do with an organized life anyway? Everyone in the film is broke. The cars, the buildings, the clothes, and the furnishings are all shabby. The economy seems to rely on the sale of used books, street-vended political T-shirts, a loose bartering system, and the kindness of strangers. No one onscreen obsesses over expensive novelties. Guys fix their cars themselves. They collect used TVs. Everyone bums cigarettes off everyone else or begs for change in the street. People try to make the most of what they have; there's no peacocking of precious polished products.

When I was a Ph.D. student, I had a meeting with my adviser—an incomparably cool professor with long, white hair who was a fan of '70s prog rock—and I told him with confidence about all the projects I was working on, the publications I was preparing, the conferences I was attending, etc., etc., etc., and he looked me straight in the eye and gave me the best advice I ever got: "Christy, don't get too corporate." Don't be mistaken: he's not the type of academic who believes capitalism is the devil. He takes a more moderate stance on that issue. For him, "Don't get too corporate" didn't really mean "Don't buy or consume stuff"; he meant it in a much more metaphorical sense. He meant, "Don't let yourself be sucked into a system that makes you base your self-worth on what you have to show for it." He meant, "Don't trade listable accomplishments for objectiveless reflection; don't believe that a full CV equals a full heart and head. The value of things worth having is unquantifiable." While most of the *Slacker* characters are explicitly and vehemently anticapitalist, I think they would be sympathetic to my adviser's less ideological counsel. One can resist the urge to bureaucratize one's life. One can refuse the busywork meant to distract from the things that actually matter. Privileging the undulating line over the straight one can free you from someone else's orthodox program of life.

Finally, a contemporary viewer might be appalled by the hygienic practices (or lack thereof) in *Slacker*. The film is full of sweaty armpits, stained T-shirts, greasy hair, and un-sterilized contact with strangers. For instance, a man licks the wrist of a woman he doesn't know at the entrance of a bar in order to transfer the PAID COVER stamp from his own wrist to hers so she can get in free. In one scene, a character tries to sell a Madonna Pap smear to some casual acquaintances she meets on the street. Many of the scenes take place in coffee shops, where the real thinking and conversation used to happen before the advent of the laptop. Now, thinking still happens in coffee shops, but it is rarely thought for thought's sake; rather, it is thinking as a means to an end, the necessary precondition for some work- or school-related achievement. In one scene, a man shows up at a coffee shop in a bathrobe. In another, the barista pulls an espresso shot with a cigarette hanging out of his mouth. Could you imagine how people would react today if this were to happen in a Starbucks? The prophylactic defensiveness of living habits now means we're safe but isolated, clean but not really alive. Pink Floyd's lyrics to "Mother" foretold all of this. The Mother, who in our time is a helicopter mom or a figure for the sanitizing State or the cleansing Corporation, will "check out all your girlfriends for you," impeding the dirty ones from getting in your life and in your trousers. She will wait up for you; she will surveil you; she will keep you laundered and unlascivious. She will muffle your libido with her love. She castrates her daughters as well as her sons. Her maternal violence is the permanent shadow over the lives of her progeny. She doesn't hesitate to show her children that she can transform into Medea if she needs to.

This song encapsulates all of the nuisances of sterile America: surveillance, hygiene, infantilization, and living programmed by someone other than ourselves. The grime of *Slacker* and the characters' response to it illustrate the possibility of survival (and, dare I say, joyful thriving?) in a dirty world. They do not fret about dust. They don't feel the need to bleach their T-shirts. And I don't get the sense that it is a feigned dirtiness, either. It's not as if they add extra mess to their lives as ornamentation; they just let the naturally arriving mess stay awhile. These characters today would probably be treated as lepers, even if there's nothing more organic than a person bearing visible and smellable traces of having moved about in the world.

A final point about the title of the film: these characters are only slackers insofar as they disregard the American Protestant work ethic narrative and take little interest in the quest to be self-made people. Though they are slackers as defined by this framework (many do not have paying jobs), they are producers of ideas, criticisms, theories, music, literature, films, and art. They toy with thoughts and try to make something out of what little they have. One could certainly argue that the characters embody white privilege, as they could be taken for well-educated people from financially comfortable families who could afford to finance their kids' drifting years. These characters don't contribute to bettering society; they simply sit around philosophizing about nothing. But a dismissal of this lifestyle is an impoverished conception of what counts as human ingenuity. The characters simply use their time to think, an activity that has far too little value in a social structure where productivity equals success. At a minimum, they are not hurting anyone or destroying anything.

They don't seem to be mooching off the system; kind people and networks of friends and roommates seem glad to help. These figures are not game changers. The world will probably continue to look the same as it always did once they are gone. But there is beauty in leaving things alone. They lead the kind of life that does not tamper with civilization, striving endlessly for the next product, invention, or innovation, tearing down what used to be. *Slacker* challenges the workaholic improvement culture that is such an integral part of the American mythology. The most important part of the slacker lifestyle depicted in the film is the pre-narcissistic moment it preserves. Slackers are not interested in self-advancement. They are not overly confident about their specialness or their singularity; they think in terms of community, despite their apparent idiosyncrasies. These figures do not exhibit the tendency toward self-obsession that is so widespread today. Instead, they think outside themselves, helping out a stranger for no reason and with nothing to gain from it. They are curious about the world outside, talking to one another, reading newspapers and books, asking questions about things with which they will never come into direct contact. There is actual fellowship in their world. The public space is a meeting place, not a venue where the digital lonelies make a fruitless public appearance.

Regardless of whether you loved or hated the movie, it is a document of something that has nearly been lost. There is something unfortunate about the fact that our consumerist, progress-obsessed, clean culture has diminished some of the variety of human typology. There is no question that this kind of person has become more scarce since the '90s; after all, why would people sport KEEP AUSTIN WEIRD bumper stickers on their cars there if there were no assault against Austin's weirdness? (Sadly, this bumper sticker exists for other American capitals of the strange: Berkeley, Eugene, Portland, Ann Arbor, Santa Cruz, Madison, etc.) After my generation dies—the last generation that knew what life felt like without the Internet—nothing except films like this will serve as remnants of a kind of living more invested in the unkempt, beautiful, meaningful marks of life than in an existence spent annihilating dirt and danger.

Through the examples I've given—Mac versus PC and *Slacker*—a set of pressing questions presents itself. Should we bid farewell to risk and let someone else manage all life on our behalf? Should we give up our ability to get our hands dirty? Do we prefer every aspect of our lives to slide smoothly along one clean, digital arc? Do we hand over our autonomy to someone who can do things for us neatly, which eventually erases our agency as individuals? Or do we prefer to stay anchored in the real and grungy world, keeping technology visible and thus external, accepting the risk and instability it brings but saving our sovereignty as people? Do we become the machine or do we use it? Do we want security or freedom? Risk or comfort? Smoothness or roughness? Sterility or dirt? Safe solitude or precarious togetherness? My intuitions favor a world in which skin still has its own smell and life is not simply something to be managed. The human is a terrestrial creature, made of *humus* or earth. We'll end down in the dirt someday. There is little reason to spend life making enemies with the soil, which occasioned—and which will eventually welcome—every body.

Southern Niceness

Southern Niceness is an expression used by my German boyfriend to describe the attitude with which I approach the world. He means it alternately as a compliment and an insult. At times, he says with admiration, "Aw, you were so nice to that lady," as though I'd far exceeded the standard courtesy threshold. Other times, he grumbles, "Why were you so nice to that lady?" after said lady was rude or unfriendly. My niceness dispensation always operates at a steady level, swayed very little by the circumstances under which I dispense it. Southern Niceness is a way to polish over the abrasive surfaces in life, but it also tries to smooth over surfaces better left rough. This attitude, which wants to avoid unpleasantness at all costs, sometimes ends up causing unpleasantness to double or triple or even to spiral into a decades-long downward corkscrew of pure animosity. Being too nice has caused me endless embarrassments and misunderstandings, particularly when this niceness was deployed outside the genteel South, where people usually understand what these gestures are all about.

In case you haven't noticed, the Civil War never ended. The South never recovered a healthy measure of self-respect after its defeat, and we're all still feeling the effects of this lack of recovery. (This wound has been exploited in many ways, like Nixon's Southern strategy, which sought to stoke white, Southern anger in order to get more votes.) Blacks in the South—and, frankly, in most of the U.S.—have never been entirely accepted as full citizens and compatriots. As long as these wounds remain—in the Southern heart and in the black heart—that nineteenth-century war will linger. I've determined that my soul is Californian, which is neither Northern nor Southern and which puts me in a position to look toward the North and the South—I've lived in both places—and think more clearly about the frictions between them. I speak on behalf of Southerners when I say that there is a persistent Northern disdain toward the South that makes us feel subhuman, underdeveloped, culturally backward, poor, and stupid. And I speak on behalf of Northerners when I say that the South projects onto us an untrue picture of godless, urban, rich, cold, and calculating elitists. (Go to a large city in the South or a rural area in the North, and much of this mythology dissipates.) The Norths and Souths of the world engage in similar conflicts, always seeing the Other as potentially dangerous. There is truth and untruth in every stereotype; your background informs your life but doesn't dictate it. I often find myself in the position of defending the South to Northerners and defending the North to Southerners. Pretend life is a macrocosmic debate club in which you have to defend positions you wouldn't pick on your own. Assign yourself the task of vindicating the person most existentially remote from you. Live hypothetically and drill yourself, in good faith, on how you might feel differently if *the completely arbitrary existence you were given belonged to somebody else.* If you are a Southerner of privilege, what can you know about being poor in the North? If you are a genius from the Midwest, what do you know about being a person with developmental difficulties in Pakistan? If you'd been born in Riyadh, would you still be a Christian? How does it feel to be Hispanic in East Texas? Chinese in Mississippi? White in Watts? A West Virginian transplanted to Chicago? A Jew in Boise?

I admit regretfully that I hide my Southern accent when in the company of East Coast scholars. Legitimacy seems easier to attain without the tensile diphthongs. My efforts at concealment are of little avail; they detect the accent anyway. A new Northern acquaintance recently said, with a bemused face, "I'm just going to make a wild guess that you're from the South," as if to say, "If you think for one second that you're fooling anybody, you're terribly mistaken."

Most find the twang delightful and ask me to say more things so they can have a little taste of sweet, sun-tea talk. I do the same thing to my coworkers from New Jersey. We just take turns asking each other to say things and then titter gleefully at the alien beauty we hear in the other's diction. After I've spent a week or so back home in Texas, the accent thickly bubbles right up. Some people I know there truly sound like

Boomhauer from *King of the Hill*, and it isn't uncommon for me to translate from Texan English to standard English when someone from out of town is visiting.

Of late, I've been using explicitly Southern phrasings in order to resist my tendency to hide. For example, I use "y'all" at the university now. "Y'all" is not grammatically incorrect. Anyone who knows a language with a second-person plural pronoun can confirm this: "Y'all" is the equivalent of *vous* (plural) in French, *voi* in Italian, *vosotros* in Spanish, and *ihr* or *Sie* (plural) in German. It's a pity that Southernness is so often equated with stupidity. My brother and I used to drive our mother nuts by saying things like, "I ain't got no home-work," which we knew was incorrect but which we used just to push her buttons. She hated the dumbness conveyed by this kind of bad grammar. I'd like to incorporate some of the colorful expressions my grandma uses—like "That boy could talk the horns off a billy goat" or "That baby is ten kinds of ugly"—but these would be inauthentic appropriations since I never talked that way. One by one, these delicious expressions fall away like wilted petals. I wish language were truly cumulative, piling up layer after layer without ever needing to get rid of anything. Why must we forget?

A long time ago, I was sitting in the trailer home of a woman I knew through an ex of mine. You could hear the locusts outside scattered in the desolate heat, hiding loudly in oak trees. I noticed that her son—who, I learned later, was in the KKK—was not around, which was strange because he usually was. "He's in jail again," she answered casually when I asked about him. "What for?" I pursued, not really wanting to know the answer. "For being ornery," she replied, lighting up a cigarette. I was curious now. "Ornery in what way?" I pressed. "He pushed his pregnant girlfriend from a moving truck." The smoke wafted up in a thin stream and the locusts kept humming. Ornery: a Southern Niceness euphemism for dark things.

Don't listen to what anybody says: New Yorkers are gentle sweethearts. (They're viciously aggressive.) They aren't loud, they aren't rude, they won't take your wallet. (They're very loud and they'll bully you on the street.) They sometimes hold the door for you and do nice things for no reason. They are proud like Texans, obviously about different things. (They will push you on the stairs roughly with their elbows.) They want to tell you about the neighborhood where they grew up and they will toss change into the guitar case of the hardworking subway musician. (They will steal the musician's earnings.) They'll hand you the glove you accidentally dropped (and tell you to go to hell) and smile (and flip you off) and tell you you're beautiful (and try to steal your backpack) and offer free hugs and paint a beautiful mural (and spray-paint over it with profanity). New Yorkers are everybody, simultaneously.

Southern Niceness has many forms: warmth of speech and action, care baked into a homemade cobbler, and unrestrained sentimentality. It's fading a little, though. People hold doors less for others than they used to. They don't say "sir" and "ma'am" as often (I feel all stiff now because I continue to use these phrases, especially with people over fifty). They won't strike up a conversation with a stranger like in the old days. Those are the fading, soft sides of Southern Niceness. But it has other dimensions, too. Sometimes, it keeps people from being critical when they should be. This is the main critique from my boyfriend. He noticed that sometimes. Southern Niceness sets up an unintended barricade of communication and action. It is fair to say that Germans are, in general, more critical than Americans. They are direct, they tell people when they are wrong, and they do not allow politeness or social niceties to keep them from saying what they think. If you are a nice American and you haven't met many Germans, go ahead and introduce yourself. It will be a learning experience. I spend much of my time in the company of Germans now, and I've learned how to be much more forthright in my self-expression because of it. Politeness is important, but it should never prevent a person from doing and saying what is morally right. (The Germans' history makes the young ones there particularly vehement about calling people out when they begin to stray ethically. Paradoxically, contemporary Germany is one of the few places in the world where another Holocaust is now almost impossible. Nearly everywhere else, genocide is always a very real possibility.) Perhaps people in the North see Southern Niceness as a kind of passive aggression, a way to cover violence with a veil of hospitality. The Moroccan writer Tahar Ben Jelloun wrote a book called *French Hospitality* (*L'Hospitalité française*) about the treatment of North African immigrants in France, posing many of the same questions: How does hospitality work, especially when it serves as a buffer between groups who view each other with suspicion? How does one welcome the stranger in more than just a superficial way? How can hospitality be duplicitous? How can someone change their own idea of who counts as an outsider?

In the South, I've heard the nicest old ladies say the most racist things, not so much out of hatred but with the automaticity of a person who'd heard this word her whole life. She speaks with a kind of matter-of-factness, in the same tone you'd use to talk about the weather. What do you say to a polite, ninety-year-old lady who says "nigger"? Do you yell? Do you lecture her or refuse to speak to her? Do you gently explain what's wrong with her word? How do you approach someone like this who is more or less from another dimension, as alien to you as a Saturnian?

The first time I ever heard an anti-Semitic slur was in a bus in France back in the '90s. In fact, every anti-Semitic slur I've ever heard—and I've heard many—was in France. (Although the South has the reputation of being anti-Semitic, I've never heard anyone openly use such slurs there. If people do things that are insensitive to Jews and people of other religions, like posting "Merry Christmas" and "Happy Easter" stuff all over the public space, it seems less a conscious dig at other faiths and more a naive assumption that everybody in America is Christian. Or at least this used to be the case; I think now there are people inspired by a made-for-TV "War on Christmas" who use "Merry Christmas" as a kind of protectionist provocation.) When I heard that first anti-Semitic slur from two aggressive, drunk men in the back of the bus, I got furious and told the person I was with to say something, my French not being good enough yet to admonish anyone convincingly. My acquaintance, a fifty-year-old homeless man who was living in the youth hostel where I worked, told me to relax and stop being so American about it. "But why should anyone have the right to be so dumb without any account-ability?" I asked in fumbled French. "That's just how it is," he answered. I experienced this kind of stuff again and again in France: in Paris, people making slanty eyes with their fingers at my boyfriend at the time, who was Asian; talking condescendingly toward my African friends in a city in the Loire Valley; using blatant housing discrimination against some Spanish and Moroccan friends of mine. And I experi-enced this in Texas, too. "Wetback" is an omnipresent word. Starting during Desert Storm, Arabs became "towel heads" or "camel jockeys," and things got much uglier after 9/11. I was once taking a walk with my friend from Togo along the road and someone called me a nigger lover out of the window of their truck. What's funny is that most people who bellow these inanities have no idea what it's like to be foreign, or not white, or different from the dominant culture in what-ever way. Go to another country where you don't speak the language and be vulnerable for a while before you open your face. It takes very little imagination to understand that if you hate someone across the globe whom you've never met, you are more or less the equivalent of that person who hates you back without having met you. Reciprocal ignorance.

Country music from my childhood has an inexplicable power over my psyche. The voice of George Jones sends me off to some inconsolable place. Don Williams's lyrics lacer-ate my solace: "Nothing makes a sound in the night like the wind does / But you ain't afraid if you're washed in the blood like I was" or "I can still hear the soft Southern winds in the live oak trees." Sometimes, I listen to old country songs on repeat in order to purge some melancholy that has welled up inside. There is a propensity in the Southern soul for suffering. Sorrow on a warm night or on a humid afternoon is the most desolate kind of sorrow. There is a very deep, unresolved misery in the South that leads toward self-destruction. Again, Don Williams knows how to put words to this misery: "When I was in school, I ran with a kid down the street / But I watched him burn himself up on bourbon and speed." I wonder what the Russian who drinks vodka until he can't see straight and the meth addict in San Antonio have in common. Once, in Dublin, I crossed the paths of several young men, each stumbling alone through the streets, the edges of their eyes tinged red with alcoholism already at nineteen years old. I think it was a Monday morning, not even eleven yet. World pain: why does it crop up where it does? Is it just an economic question? If every numbing substance—alcohol, drugs, cigarettes, fatty food, porn—just vanished into thin air across the planet, what would become of us? What if the guns and knives fell to pieces like rust? What if the muscles needed for fist clenching no longer worked? The South is a miniaturized tableau of human misery on a global scale. Southern suffering is universal. The South itself is an elegy.

Brutality and love live in holy matrimony. Southern Niceness offsets Southern Meanness. For every sour thing our universe exudes, a sweet thing is there to meet it. Look up where the word "nice" came from. It originally meant foolish, silly, ignorant, needy, unaware, and clumsy. Even language offers up a yin for every yang.

I am writing another book at the same time as I'm writing this one, a book on the theme of rootedness. This troublesome metaphor, which people use to describe their firm attachment to places, tempts me for personal reasons: I am deeply conflicted about my roots. I can never live in the place I came from, and yet every time I return for a visit, I am filled for the first few days with euphoric nostalgia, which inevitably turns into something resembling despair. I have such a deep love and appreciation for North Texas and the people and landscape that form its character, I can barely find words for it. But ever since I left and looked around the world a bit, I continue to recognize the unbearably high degree of despondency and apprehension there, which I never would have noticed if I hadn't looked at it from the outside. Much of the pain there is self-inflicted. But pain is always the product of a history, either genealogical or societal. Why all the fear and anger? Is it much older than the soul-dividing Civil War? Did the fear and anger arrive on boats and in wagons?

Some people believe that the land and climate are prime factors in the development of a culture's character. If you've ever been in Texas between May and October, you understand that the sun isn't that interested whether you live or die. The snakes and scorpions and wasps and spiders that live there are symbols of bad-assery for a reason. During a recent visit, my mom and I were looking in our front yard at an armadillo, which more or less resembles a small dinosaur. You see armadillos dead along the highway—they are no match for the myriad F-150s that plow down I-35 at ninety miles an hour—but for that reason, they are perfect symbols of people run into the ground by a certain kind of hopeless consumerism despite their tough exteriors. For those who are just scraping by, "Big D" no longer means Dallas; it means Big Debt. And financial desperation leads to other kinds of desperation. People get restless and agitated; politics get weird; numbing is needed in any form. And I watch it all from afar and I ache. My roots are in an injured soil.

This year, I've been living in New Haven, Connecticut, where just as much if not more desperation exists, but of a very different kind. The presence of Yale University there makes the contrast between the haves and the have-nots all the more conspicuous. The particularly harsh winter this year pushed everyone out of public view over several months. Problems were covered by the snowfall. The richness or poorness of bundled-up people is less easily discerned. Maybe because they were hidden for a good part of the year, the poverty and addictions and abuses in New Haven seemed somehow reparable. Spring arrived—very late—and the people came out and there was some joy in their faces, even the most destitute among them. The homeless have a social community; they call each other by name, and they are friendly with the bus drivers and the people who sell lighters and sunglasses from fold-up tables on the street. But back home in Texas, there is no such consolation, even in the mild winter. And in the summer, the heat can make even the most delicate soul begin to rage. It is impossible to think clearly. Life becomes an extended act of self-flagellation, something to endure, if only just barely. People have lost all confidence in life and look for ways to leave it in a blaze of glory. I've never been able to locate the source of this absolute non-hope, but it creeps into your subconscious, even if you're there for only ten days.

I wonder if New Haven seems better off because it has

an urban center. People are pressed into a compact space but are not as faceless or nameless as they might be in New York or Chicago. In Texas, outside its few large cities, everything is spread out wide along the prairie. There isn't much public transportation anywhere. If you don't have a car, you mostly stay put. People walk along the mirage-emitting cement, along the dead grass that catches fire from cigarettes thrown out of the windows of cars with no air-conditioning. You sometimes see a woman with no teeth wearing an oversize T-shirt and flip-flops by herself under a bridge, and you know she is a prostitute with a meth habit. You hear about kids you went to school with, now in jail for murder or themselves victims of murder. At night, people get ornery in bar parking lots. There are guns and there is anger. I've often wondered, were great metropolises the size of New York City suddenly to spring up all over the South and grow suburbs out of their centers, if things would change any. Would cities spawn the kind of togetherness you see sometimes in New Haven or would violence and anguish surge? A city certainly wouldn't make the heat go away. That heat is like Colonel Kurtz's horror at the end of *Heart of Darkness*. You cannot put your finger on it, yet it is everywhere and no one is exempt from it. That heat unhinges the psyche. And when you go into a restaurant or a bank, air-conditioned to the same temperature as a meat locker, you freeze and shudder until the automatic doors slide open and the heat punches you in your trembling gut. Southern logic is a logic of extremes.

But maybe the South is only a metaphor for a certain set of values. In his song "A Country Boy Can Survive," one of my favorites growing up, Hank Williams Jr. gathers the rural geographies of the United States into a cohesive "we":

"We came from the West Virginia coalmines and the Rocky Mountains and the western skies [. . .] We're from North California and South Alabam', and little towns all around this land." What if "Southern" is just a code word for rural? I saw a twentysomething guy here in Connecticut a few weeks back with a huge Confederate flag flying behind his monster truck, along with a black "Don't Tread on Me" flag. He had a Connecticut license plate. The South isn't just a place; it's a mind-set.

A strange coincidence: for my project on roots, I was reading a staggering book from 1980 called *Le Corps noir* (*The Black Body*) by a Haitian writer named Jean-Claude Charles. He coined the term *enracinerrance*, a French neologism that fuses the idea of rootedness and wandering. He spent his life between Haiti, New York, and Paris, very comfortably rooted in his nomadism. The first line of one of his experimental chapters is this: "il était une fois john howard griffin mansfield texas" ("once upon a time there was john howard griffin in mansfield texas"). I was stunned to find the small town that shares a border with my hometown in the pages of this Haitian author's book published in France. What in the world was Mansfield, Texas, doing in this book I'd found by chance while researching roots for a totally unrelated academic project? The white man named John Howard Griffin referred to by Charles had conducted an experiment back in the late 1950s in which he disguised himself as a black man in order to understand what it must feel like to be black in the South. He darkened his skin with an ultraviolet lamp and skin-darkening medication and then took to the road, confirming the daily abuses in the South toward people with more melanin in their skin. His experiences were compiled in the classic *Black Like Me* (1962), which was later made into a film. When the book came out, Griffin and his family in Mansfield received death threats. It is astounding that I found out about this experiment, which began one town over from mine, through a gleefully nomadic Haitian who slipped it into his pain-filled essay about the black body. If you don't return to your roots, they come and find you.

I refuse to stop being nice. And my Southernness is also part and parcel of my person, so it stays, too. I've chosen the donkey as my totem animal because it is gentle, humble, and stubborn. Perhaps it is a figure for the South, too: a beast of burden that is obstinate but naturally good-natured. The donkey is the symbol of the Democrats, a witness to the Nativity, Winnie-the-Pooh's dejected companion, and the patron saint of the *Jackass* franchise. Many different ideas have been projected onto this animal—including my belief that it is a graceful and modest creature. People always project human characteristics onto animals, either to bring them closer to us or to push them farther away. Humans feel plain lonely in the universe and constantly seek a cure for this loneliness: gods, aliens, angels, ghosts, pets, plants we can talk to, virtual avatars, the talking glove in Hamburger Helper commercials, or other objects that speak. We can't bear to be alone. But there are plenty of people on the planet who, if figurative and literal borders were more permeable, might have a few nice things to say to one another, diminishing some of the solitude. The courteous reputation of the South—as much a projection as the humanlike aspects of the donkey—is not so much false as it is complicated. There are very real historical reasons for

Southern Niceness and for those aspects of Southern culture that put everyone else on edge. Niceness comes at a price. It is certainly part of a coping mechanism, a way to make the hard parts of life more manageable. But it can have a much darker side, which leads to the neglect of pressing problems or helps maintain a disastrous kind of pride. Awful things are often done politely. I suppose we have to think about the difference between niceness-as-form and niceness-as-content. Is Southern Niceness an empty gesture, like asking, "How are you?" without really caring to know the answer? Or is it a very full gesture that says, "I am decent and I want to join the world with good will," but that doesn't know how to dispense with the centuries of wounded pride, derision, and the incapacity to change course? It is both, of course. Everything is always both, hovering between extremes and drifting toward one pole or the other as years pass and as the earth spins.

On Awkwardness

Never give a sword to a man who can't dance.

—Celtic proverb, allegedly

People have been awkward at least since the middle of the fourteenth century when the word was coined in English. It means "moving in the wrong direction" (like "northward," but awk + ward), zigging when a zag is in order. Even the spelling of "awkward" is awkward if you stare at the "k" sandwiched between two "w's."

Awkwardness is the bête noire of the contemporary American soul. It is to be avoided at all costs, and people will go to great lengths to be sure that their interpersonal encounters contain as little awkwardness as possible. This is why breaking up via text message is such a useful innovation; it lets you skirt that twitchy moment of definitive separation. At the same time, awkwardness is one of the most turned-to sources for entertainment, inside or outside the media; there is something delightfully painful about witnessing awkward scenes. In his book *Awkwardness*, Adam Kotsko takes a celebratory position toward the phenomenon, tracing its history and philosophical underpinnings in Western culture and identifying its function in popular cinema and television. While it is nice to see someone embrace the concept as potentially productive for the human psyche, I want to think through its ubiquity in America and piece together the possible repercussions for a populace that simultaneously avoids and steeps itself in this kind of social discomfort.

A sharp student of mine named Gabriella has a compelling theory about awkwardness. She says that when a person describes another as awkward—or that other favorite buzzword today, "creepy"—it only means that the accuser is unable to manage the social situation at hand. It's not that there are suddenly throngs of awkward, creepy people everywhere; it's that we know less and less how to deal with even the most basic negotiations necessary for face-to-face interaction. Circumstances that twenty years ago would have been viewed as coming with the territory of talking to another human being are now considered "awkward" or "weird" or "uncomfortable." Anything that doesn't cleanly fit into a prescripted expressive category is automatically regarded with suspicion.

There are many opportunities for awkwardness: misplaced silences, bad timing, miscommunications, accidental encounters, speaking too soon or too late, mismanaging one's body, or failing to understand how to approach a particular social moment. Awkwardness lurks around every corner.

An unequivocally social phenomenon, it requires at least two people in order to happen. Could you imagine a new kind of awkwardness that involved only a single individual? This could be the basis for the great American novel of the twenty-first century: a protagonist who, in complete solitude, makes herself repeatedly uncomfortable even outside the social sphere.

There are some interesting synonyms for "awkward," but they never quite do justice to the all-encompassing concept: inept, bungling, clumsy, unskillful, heavy-handed, tactless, undiplomatic, inconsiderate, incompetent, klutzy, inelegant, unsophisticated, cumbersome, unwieldy, ungainly, graceless, blundering, gawky. I like the expressions "all thumbs," "butterfingered," and especially "ham-fisted." Some of these terms describe a person; others, an action. But "awkward" is the best catchall word to describe an individual, a circumstance, a sentence, or even the uncomely fit of a piece of clothing.

"Awkward" is sometimes difficult to translate into other languages. In French, you have *maladroit* and *gauche* (which means "left"), both of which have made their way into English. The latter hints at a kind of social incompetence while the former seems to imply a lack of physical proficiency. To describe an awkward conversation, the French use the adjective *délicat* or maybe *gênant* (embarrassing). In Italian, you have words like *goffo, impacciato*, and *sgraziato*, which all imply a physical clumsiness or lack of grace. To describe an awkward phase, like adolescence, Italians use words such as *problematico, difficile*, or *complicato*, whose equivalents in English don't get anywhere near the efficient beauty of "awkward." In Spanish, there's *torpe*, which shares an etymological root with the English "torpor" and implies numbness, or *des-*

mañado, which suggests that the person is not good with his hands. In German, an object that is *unhandlich* is not easily handled. There's also *ungeschickt* (which refers to the fact that fate, *das Geschick*, doesn't come to your aid), *unbeholfen* (that you can't be helped), *linkisch* ("leftish," like *gauche* in French, as in having two left feet), and *tölpelhaft* (like a clumsy sea-bird). My favorite is *tollpatschig*, a word borrowed from the Hungarian word for foot soldier. Apparently, Hungarian foot soldiers in the seventeenth century often had no shoes so instead strapped soles directly to their feet with strings, which made them walk in a funny way. Austrians were the first to use this as a derogatory term to describe a clumsy person. It's notable that in English and other languages, the feet and hands are so important to the concept of awkwardness. These appendages can be the biggest nuisance in the management of one's environment. Hands and feet, the body's tools for doing and for going, are often the primary impediments to physical competence. The faux pas, or false step, brings about the social tumble.

The limbs and tongue compete to embarrass the person who owns them. In Italy once, I meant to order an espresso and a croissant (*un cornetto*), but instead ordered an espresso and a man whose wife sleeps around (*un cornuto*). In high school and later, I attended many of my brother's heavy metal shows—he is a drummer, the kind who breaks sticks and obliterates drumheads—which caused, I believe, some hearing loss. For this reason, I am always speaking too quietly or too loudly and I have to ask people to repeat what they've already said multiple times. Furthermore, I move according to the laws of vaudeville. I run into things. I forget the dimensions of my body and bump into easily avoidable, breakable obstacles. My three-dimensional vision is deficient: I notice this most when trying to parallel park, never sure at all of the size of my vehicle even though it sits plainly in sight around me. The car balloons into a massive object or shrinks to miniature proportions when I look at its contours through the rearview mirror, but it never seems to me the size it actually is.

I've been told by friends and acquaintances that my walk is ridiculous. I have a sort of bouncing, elastic gait to my step even when moving slowly. Some say I move belly first in a weird kind of slouch. Others have noticed I have a hard time moving in straight lines. Some claim I drag my heels. Still others have identified an awkward smoothness in the way I still roll my feet as I learned to do in marching band. How can a person bounce, slouch, swerve, drag, and roll all at the same time? I don't know, but that's the only way I know how to describe my walk. I could have interned at Monty Python's Ministry of Silly Walks. My boyfriend calls me "gazelle."

The moment your walk is called to your attention, you become hyper self-conscious about it. Your gait changes instantly. I have yet to catch a pure sample of myself walking; as soon as I pay attention to my walk, it becomes something very different from what it was. Most people are highly recognizable by how they walk. It's one of those signature features of the human. I had a professor once who walked like a slow-moving waterbird, the stately and long-legged kind, like a flamingo or a heron. Her gait was quicker, but the mechanics were definitely avian and of the aquatic variety. You could identify her in a crowd from three acres away by her strutting head. She traversed campus as though it were a marsh. A friend of mine claims she can recognize everyone she knows based solely on the sound of their steps. Each person is marked by a singular peripatetic cadence: swish-clop-swish, scuff-scuff-scuff, tip-tap-tip-tap. The rhythm of one's feet is a kind of identity metronome.

Tripping and falling are great comedic resources. The French philosopher Henri Bergson had a theory about why we laugh about tripping and other such forms of awkwardness. He argued that when people are too trapped in the automaticity of their mechanical movements and when these are insufficient in dealing with the environment at hand, a comical situation presents itself. Bound by the habits of movement, people sometimes forget to adjust for new terrain or unexpected obstacles, or they get so accustomed to their standard environment, they expect the body to do all the work intuitively. This overreliance on the bodily mechanism leads to a farcical malfunction. Slapstick is not just for the Three Stooges; physical comedy is a free, renewable resource available for mining from that generous repository, the body. I often daydream about falling down in front of large crowds of people, usually walking toward the podium at an important conference in front of illustrious colleagues and biting the dust as hard as one possibly can, grabbing at whatever is closest to keep from falling, which happens to be the sleeve of the tweed blazer of a renowned specialist of twentieth-century French literature, which rips emphatically in the silence of the startled conference hall. Or I jolt the table in front of the panelists waiting to give their talks and spill Dasani on their crotches. In some versions, my shoe flies in an unnatural direction, as if my fall caused physics to undo itself momentarily. Or I knock out my front teeth on the lectern. I've mentally rehearsed all the possible scenarios of this second Fall of Woman.

Tripping is the great equalizer. When you are intimidated by someone, it is helpful to imagine either what this person was like when they were seven years old or what they look like when they lose their footing on the stairs. Either way, the hidden vulnerabilities of the intimidating individual are exposed, making them human and fallible like everyone else. The fact that we all can fall creates proximity between the most disparate types of people. It works like the allegorical *danse macabre* frescoes painted on the walls of medieval churches, which show death in a dance with people of all social ranks, a depiction of death's universality. Tripping is like death; not one of us is exempt from it.

An interesting if little-known fact: the etymological origin of the word "scandal" means a trap or a stumbling block intended to hinder an enemy. The scandal is that which trips up one's social life. The awkwardness of political scandals, especially those of a sexual nature, comes from the public visibility of the secret part of someone's life. When the private becomes public, awkwardness is always a possibility. Intimate life is generally carried out with the understanding that there is no audience (outside the intended one) to bear witness to the confidential palette of one's desires. When this expectation is frustrated by public exposure, one is transformed into the deer in the proverbial headlights. The reflex is to cover up quickly, but this is a hopeless impulse. Once the image of someone's tweeted junk is flashed before the public, it is etched with an acid quill on the surface of the brain. Like the blood on the hands of Lady Macbeth, the picture is indelible even once the tangible object is no longer visible. Such awkwardnesses cannot be effaced. I predict that the threat of blackmail will be much less effective in the not-so-distant future since people will be more and more aware that their own digital goings-on have the potential to be hacked and exposed. The thrill of seeing it happen to someone else will decrease with this knowledge. Someone else's exposure will make you think increasingly of your own exposure and thus the revelation of naughtiness will lose its appeal as a source of entertainment. The power of this kind of blackmailing will dwindle since an indecorous picture will no longer trigger public indignation.

In Milan Kundera's *The Art of the Novel*, in a chapter called "Sixty-three Words," he writes an entry on the word "obscenity," noting the difficulty of seducing a woman with obscene words in a language that isn't your own. If you've had lovers who didn't have a strong command of your language but tried to seduce you with it anyway, you understand this farcical scenario, which turns the flushed skin of passion into the flushed skin of embarrassment. Sex has a highly systematized vocabulary and grammar. While the foreign accent can triple or sextuple a person's appeal, the misuse of a preposition can cause the whole thing to come crashing down. Using an idiomatic expression that doesn't exist in the target language—"I want to butter your biscuits"—induces more laughter than desire.

Italo Calvino's *Mr. Palomar* chisels out a long shoreline of awkwardness. The protagonist is out of sync with the world, fumbling at life because of his tendency to overthink. In a chapter called "The Naked Bosom," Mr. Palomar comes across a topless sunbather on the beach. Confronted with the non-neutral fullness of the female form, he deliberates how he should behave in this encounter. Should he ignore her, as if she were part of the scenery? Should he "create a kind of mental brassière" to keep his eyes from grazing her breasts? Or should he acknowledge that her body is beautiful by looking at it unambiguously, as one would a flower? He vacillates, pacing and wondering what to do, which disturbs the woman, causing her to pack up her things quickly and leave, "as if she were avoiding the tiresome insistence of a satyr." This is only one of his countless indiscretions. When in the company of others, he has purposely developed the habit of biting his tongue three times before saying anything, to avoid saying something stupid. Palomar is an observer; he walks through the world noticing in particular those elements of life that are slightly off-kilter, like himself. He loves to watch giraffes race at the zoo, admiring their "unharmonious movements": "The giraffe seems a mechanism constructed by putting together pieces from heterogeneous machines, though it functions perfectly all the same." He watches the clumsy mating ritual of two tortoises who fumble at love, making it impossible for an outside observer to tell if their lurching and slow acrobatics were the picture of successfully choreographed coitus. Palomar even turns stargazing into an awkward affair through overpreparedness, as he arms himself with star maps, a flashlight, and a deck chair. He suddenly realizes that in the dark—as he's been craning his neck, twisting and turning in his chair, fooling with his stubborn charts—he has transformed himself into a spectacle more interesting than the sidereal show above. A small crowd has gathered around him in the dimness, "observing his movements like the convulsions of a madman." Palomar is representative of our time because he is self-aware to the point of immobilizing himself. Too busy scrutinizing his every thought and action, trying to analyze and prepare himself for every possible scenario, he never does what comes naturally. His self-consciousness has made him existentially constipative. Over-enlightened thinking has cramped him up lifewise.

Over one hundred years earlier, Emerson took a different stance on the question of awkwardness. For him, its cause is too little thought. He wrote this beautiful passage in an essay called "Social Aims":

> Nature is the best posture-master. An awkward man is graceful when asleep, or when hard at work, or agreeably amused. The attitudes of children are gentle, persuasive, royal, in their games and in their house-talk and in the street, before they have learned to cringe. 'Tis impossible but thought disposes the limbs and the walk, and is masterly or secondary. No art can contravene it or conceal it. Give me a thought, and my hands and legs and voice and face will all go right. And we are awkward for want of thought. The inspiration is scanty, and does not arrive at the extremities.

At first, Emerson seems to put nature at odds with thought, since he claims that the sleeping man, in his unpondered and innate bearing, displays no awkwardness. Children, who have not yet "learned to cringe"—what a thought!—are as natural and perfectly postured as the man in slumber. Cringeworthiness is a meaningless concept to a child. But in his last sentences, we see that thought is somehow an extension of nature, a rectifying force. While Palomar is awkward in his surplus of thought, for Emerson, "we are awkward for want of thought." And here, once again, the problem of the extremities presents itself. Heady inspiration has trouble trickling down into the arms and legs. There isn't enough thought to go around. So while nature is the posture-master, the human, largely cut off from nature, relies on the brain to calibrate posture. Consciousness can program the body to move fluently. But only in sleep can we return to the fully unprogrammed, graceful state reserved for children, poplar trees, and herons.

Awkwardness triggers the biological flight response in contemporary Americans. There is something unbearable about witnessing scenarios that have moved inextricably deep into the awkward zone. It makes you want to run away. And when you can't run away, you show your discomfort visibly, which is why words like "facepalm" and "cringeworthy" have gained a lot of currency in recent years. Interestingly, for a moment to be cringeworthy, it requires you to temporarily put yourself in the place of the person who has committed the sin of awkwardness; it is an empathic response. As a witness to someone else's awkward drama, you make a sound in your head as though you have burned your own hand on a red-hot stove. (I'm not sure how to render this sound in writing. An inwardly sucked "sssssssss"?) You imagine yourself to be that guy who wanted to give a high five but was snubbed, his hand suspended dumbly in midair with no hand to answer it. Or that pageant contestant who answers a question about world affairs of grave importance with prettily spoken non-sense: you cringe at her brainlessness but you secretly know that if you were onstage in heels with lights in your face and pressure weighing on you to be perfect, all this fueled by a lifetime of weirdness that would put you on a pageant stage in the first place, you would likely have a difficult time producing a clever response. We cringe because we project ourselves into the scene, making ourselves a character in the drama of the uncomfortable. The person who made the error cringes, as do the witnesses to this error. In this mystical way, awkwardness engenders a community of the embarrassed. We recognize each other by our red faces.

Awkwardness has an ideal format: the tableau. This is what the awkward moments I've narrated so far have in common. They naturally frame themselves as scenes or events, which require three elements: a setting, a moment, and a confluence of characters. Even better is when witnesses external to the event are there to see it. For a scene to be as awkward as possi-ble, someone should behold it. For these reasons, television is a prime venue for staging awkwardness. The original British version of *The Office*, for example, got most of its comedic payoff from David Brent making others uncomfortable, in-cluding the audience. This format, the mockumentary, has proved viable for the celebration of awkwardness. *Parks and Recreation* and *Modern Family* capitalize on the possibilities of this genre, which allows the director to emphasize the awkwardness of a given exchange by zooming in on the reactions of the characters trapped in it. The shot is held just a little longer than a witness would be comfortable looking on in real life, letting at-home viewers marinate in the malaise. However, because awkwardness is a regular part of televised life in America, it has caused real-life awkwardness to lose some of its potency. Awkwardness is no longer exceptional; it is a part of everyday mediatized and non-mediatized living. Perhaps people have become more numb to embarrassment through this process. We call things awkward but don't actually feel the sting of the situation as acutely as before. Doing stupid things is now cause for celebration: YOLO. I'm not sorry. By choreographing a self-inclusive tableau of awkwardness, one successfully stages an attention-worthy scene in the endless buzz of scenes. This is why people on Facebook and Twitter often narrate stupid things they did. It is a part of self-fashioning, a way to engineer humility (as I have done in telling about my silly walk). This way, one can humanize oneself without actually enduring the painful moment of *unchosen* awkwardness. It is awkwardness, one step removed. Discomfort held at a distance. When awkwardness is mediated in some form, it is made bearable if not satisfying.

The fuel of American awkwardness is banality. The microgaffes of everyday life get an undue amount of attention because without them, minds might be at leisure to think toward much more acute humiliations. Americans are taught to be self-conscious about the wrong things. The emphasis on small embarrassments distracts from more genuine sources of shame, like ignorance about life outside the U.S. and the indefensible violence carried out on our behalf. Sheepishness provoked by insignificant social blunders invites a strange comfort, relieving the brain of more consequential thoughts. This safe irritation puts people ill enough at ease to remember they're alive and susceptible to social law but doesn't press them to recognize their role as civic agents. For this reason, it makes sense to refuse the concept of awkwardness, except on a civilizational scale. There are things to be ashamed of, but they have nothing to do with poorly timed jokes or a stumble on the steps. Catch yourself the next time you use the word "awkward"; was the sentiment merited or better saved for circumstances of a greater scale? Someone benefits from our ill-at-easeness. Just not us.

What are we to make of this ubiquity of awkwardness, in all its various degrees and settings? Is it the expression of a general sense of alienation? Because we are the only species that constantly severs ties with nature, we feel generally out of place in the world and perhaps this out-of-placeness needs a form in which to express itself. When an animal is bad at life, it simply dies. When people are bad at life, they are constantly saved by social safety nets around them, individuals and institutions who sweep in to help them through their folly. Ties have been broken with our animal selves who worried mainly about survival; the average person in America not only survives but has the time and luxury to do ridiculous, hyperconscious things. Time not spent hunting and gathering is surplus time for imbecility to flourish. Or maybe the permanent incapacity to feel at ease in the social field is due to a lack of landmarks to help us get our bearings. You can't really assume any longer that the person sitting next to you was brought up in a similar way, shares your political views, or even speaks your language. Our social intuition is out of joint because the clusters of individual experiences brought to the table are decreasingly similar. Despite the standardization of culture that happens through the consumerist project in the form of pop music, TV series, and products that uniformize collective desires and homogenize individuality, the U.S. is a much more diverse place than it was even fifty years ago. When a populace is as variegated as ours, the conditions for cultural confusion are created. Everyone now has the potential to be odd in the eyes of someone else.

America is a muddle of influences. In the 1950s, there was perhaps some standard of social behavior that worked as a code of conduct. Manners were established at home, where both parents were often present, or through church or school. Many people had more contact with others outside their own age group: sometimes three or perhaps even four generations lived under the same roof, which meant that the values of the grandparents were more easily transmitted to the grandchildren. People are now cloistered by age. Back then, the middle class was pretty big. Races mixed less; classes mixed less. There were fewer newly arrived foreigners, or at least there were foreigners from fewer places. People were trained by the historical inertia of cultural habit. All of this has changed, I think for the better. While at times it may feel destabilizing not to have a clear code of conduct in the social world, everyone is basically in the same boat. What a unifying feeling that we are all equally lost!

M_Y point is that awkwardness comes with the territory of diversity. I don't mean racial diversity or even cultural diversity, but rather, more comprehensively, the very basic diversity brought about by being a different human from someone else, that is to say, the atomization of the collective into individuals. This has been one of the principal projects of America: to elevate the individual above all other units. But at what cost? Awkwardness is the outcome of not knowing how to deal with an unfamiliar (i.e., foreign) situation. We are becoming increasingly alien to one another by virtue of the mediated existences we lead. By making everything outside the body more and more foreign, more and more remote, we cause the occasions for awkwardness to increase exponentially. Any encounter contains within it this risk. Awkwardness is about feeling out of control and incapable of maneuvering things back to a manageable state. It is produced by the anticipatory anxiety of knowing that whatever comes from outside threatens the equilibrium of the closed self.

While awkwardness is entertaining at times, it bespeaks an unnecessary anxiousness in the face of the unknown and the unknowable. Feeling ill at ease is not the only possible response to a situation in which you don't know what to do. The next time you find yourself in an awkward circumstance, imagine if you embraced fully the foreignness of the moment. You are no longer intimidated that you've never encountered this kind of moment before. You are aware of but not oversensitive to the unclearness of your role in the situation. You watch it as a detached observer. Recognize it as an occasion for thinking beyond yourself, outside your body and your routine. Be and love the alien. Can the uncanny. Realize that when it's over, it constitutes part of your broadened repertoire of experience. Remember: the "awk" in "awkward" is a fictional direction. Just assert yourself calmly in the flow of the unknown. When every possible direction is interesting, there is no such thing as waywardness.

Treat Your Country
Like Your Child,
Not Your Parent

[The] poignantly tender feeling for some beautiful, precious, fragile, and perishable object has a warmth about it which the sentiment of national grandeur altogether lacks. [. . .] A perfectly pure love for one's country bears a close resemblance to the feelings which his young children, his aged parents, or a beloved wife inspire in a man. The thought of weakness can inflame love in just the same way as can the thought of strength.

—SIMONE WEIL, *The Need for Roots*

I t's an easy mental adjustment. When you are little, your parents are omnipresent and infallible beings with absolute authority over you. You do what you're told and hold little sway. You might not even notice the big persons' flaws, but when they make mistakes, you watch and imitate, eventually becoming a miniature version of the looming figures. What they started gets perpetuated through you, as either an affirmation (mimicry) or a negation (rebellion). You understand they are your contact with a more complicated and mysterious world and put yourself willingly in your parents' care in exchange for their service as a buffer between you and harsher realities.

In the reverse situation, when you make the decision to be a parent responsibly, you enter into an implicit contract with this small being whom you *chose* to invite here. Your child's interests are your priority. Your job is to facilitate the kid's growth into the best kind of person. Since you can't selfishly expect a mere carbon copy of yourself, you celebrate the child's independence and development of a healthy body, mind, and spirit. Yours is a role of attentive interest and keen-eared, one-room-away involvement. You are not a warden; you are a provider and a teacher. You intervene to set things right when they've gone wrong, realizing your child is not blameless. If not, you are negligent. In the best-case scenario, your gestures toward your child are marked with care; apathy has no place in your role as parent. In the public space, your child is an extension of you, so you do the best you can to keep that fact from being embarrassing. When your child hits another child, takes a toy from another, or hits a dog, you intervene. And when your child helps someone, with no expectation of something in return, you feel a deep sense of pride and humility.

You see where I'm going with this. A next step in the exercise: replace "country" with "world" in the title.

The Metaphor of
Masking Tape

When I moved to California—into a white-walled, wood-floored apartment whose entryway invited guests to behold the large windows filled with splashes of leaf green, like a movie screen showing a film about West Coast flora—I saw that the wall that held those windows had to be painted orange. The citrus detail would thrill any visitor.

I bought supplies at a hardware store, staring with the usual awe at the paint-mixing machine and its epileptic pulse, too fevered and nervous a gesture for the milky pigment in the can. Back at home, I muffled the wood floor with plastic film and taped the margins of the wall, using a utility knife to perfect the imperfect lines I'd made, slicing vigilantly down the corner crease and peeling away the excess masking tape. With an amateur hand, I smeared that wall orange with a brush and a roller, taking all the liberties afforded by my adhesive ally: I leaked, dabbed, dripped, and blotted across the stretch of tape like the rookie I was. But after the paint had dried, I peeled myself into rapture, each band of tape revealing a pristine surface underneath, a harmonious encounter of orange and white. There is nothing more satisfying than the indulgent strum sound of tape ribbons peeled from plaster.

Masking tape is a product of and a remedy for human imprecision. Before the thought of it occurred to anyone, all brushstrokes that aimed for rectilinear perfection were prudent. The eye and hand had to orchestrate their movements, but even then, the quivering tics of muscles and feeble attention foiled most attempts at a clean line.

Along came masking tape. Not so sticky as to peel away paint that was already there but sticky enough to give moral support to an unsteady line, masking tape created the conditions for simultaneous messiness and order. Similar to an eraser in its function, masking tape allows for the removal of error, an effacement of the all-too-human trace.

In the old days, the professional painter lived in a constant state of precarity. The task took longer to complete and the stakes were higher. Perhaps the old painter developed the muscle memory to make a straight line in one fluid stroke. But in an apprentice, these muscles undoubtedly quivered like those of a fawn getting to its feet soon after birth. Masking tape brought the fawn a motorized scooter, allowing it to zigzag speedily to its destination, the grass covering all traces of its veering presence.

What does masking tape teach us? It values both perfection and imperfection equally. It sees nothing wrong with human fallibility. It even invites error, like the spell checker on your word processor. Happy with approximation, it never requires you to be meticulous. If you can get within the vicinity of the intended word (the polite spell check asks, "You wrote 'expresso.' Did you mean 'espresso'?"), it can help you toward correctness. The same goes for masking tape: if you keep your wobbling brush within the boundaries of the tape width (one-inch, two-inch, three-inch tape: how deep is your swerve?), the forgiving adhesive will rectify your wrongs. Masking tape accommodates restlessness and recklessness, improvisation and imperfection. Its rectification is subsequent to natural error, which it accepts on its lenient surface.

Look up the word "human" in your thesaurus. As an adjective, it is synonymous with "susceptible," "vulnerable," "fallible," "error prone," "mortal," and "imperfect." Masking tape is customized for our species, then. It lets us be what we already are. In his early-eighteenth-century "Essay on Criticism," Alexander Pope wrote, "To err is human, to forgive divine." Masking tape is the adhesive of forgiveness, a divine garland pressed along the periphery of our pieces, which it transforms into masterpieces. We are exonerated, exculpated. In its majesty, masking tape absolves the human of its humanity.

One could even look toward masking tape as a metaphor for a certain kind of living, one that appreciates messy spontaneity as well as the beauty of flawless form. Such a life would be lived in the service of unschooled impulses and intuitive gestures, but with a safety buffer, an external corrective. The notion of a mistake is negated under this philosophy. One who lives in such a way is not frozen by the paranoia about making an error. She can try out new strokes and revisit them later. These tentative marks are private; the audience is only invited to the post-peel party. Everyone is thus satisfied, the imperfect artist and her perfection-seeking public.

You Have No
Power over Me

You have no power over me: this is the phrase used by
Sarah to break the Goblin King's spell at the end of
Jim Henson's *Labyrinth* (1986). I've chosen this phrase as
my mantra because it helps to distinguish between real and
imagined oppressions. Much of our lives are spent cower-
ing in the shadow of false rulers. *Labyrinth* is an allegory of
woman's self-emancipation, which explains why a whole generation of women was stirred by the film. The film tells the
story of Sarah (Jennifer Connelly), whose half brother Toby
is stolen by the Goblin King, Jareth (David Bowie). In order
to retrieve the child, she has to solve the labyrinth that leads
to the Goblin City and to Jareth's castle, where Toby is being
held. Along the way, in a fantastical landscape full of fairies,
monsters, and other strange creatures, she makes several new

friends: Hoggle, a cowardly troll; Ludo, a gentle giant; and Sir Didymus, a chivalrous little dog who rides a bigger dog as his noble steed. Step by step, Sarah symbolically frees herself from a variety of societal impositions on women. Here are a few of them:

Sexual repression

Sarah is a fifteen-year-old girl. This is a symbolic year for young women in Latin American culture, where the *quinceañera* celebrates her initiation from girlhood into womanhood. In this ceremony, a kind of pre-wedding, the girl enters the room wearing a special dress, accompanied by her father, a symbolic husband and guardian. In *Labyrinth*, Sarah appears in a dream vision wearing what looks like a white wedding dress and ends up dancing with the Goblin King, who selects her from among countless other libidinous attendees of his masked ball. When the film was made, David Bowie was almost forty and Jennifer Connelly was around fifteen. The father-daughter incest taboo is glossed over in the film, treated as the sweet imaginings of a young girl looking for her prince (or, rather, her king). For many women born in the late 1970s and 1980s, their first on-screen love was David Bowie's character. This androgynous figure with long hair, makeup, and skintight riding pants gave us all something to dream about. He existed in a world away from parents and proprieties, a world where a girl could be a sexual being if she so chose. In her song "At Seventeen," Janis Ian sings about the ugly girls who "desperately remained at home, inventing lovers on the phone who called to say, 'Come dance with me,' and murmured vague obscenities." These are the years when girls articulate their erotic lives, at least in their minds;

but their desires are always kept in check by various societal barriers: slut shame, virgin fetishism, fear of disease, and murderous fathers who want to kill their lovers. Sarah is not interested in flesh-and-blood boys; she prefers an imaginary lover. As soon as he becomes too real, she dissolves him.

At one point, the Goblin King uses her troll friend Hoggle to get Sarah to eat a cursed peach. The scene screams original sin. While the serpent is replaced by a troll, the apple by a peach, and knowledge by forgetting, the setting is still a plant world and the result is the Fall of Woman. (When we think about the dangerous apple, it becomes clear that *Snow White*, too, is profoundly biblical.) After taking a bite, Sarah is incapacitated and dreams a crystal vision of herself in a corrupt scene of decadence and debauchery, which she ultimately refuses, fleeing this world of bodies and material excess. She doesn't want the form of sex that's been imposed on her by the enchanted fruit. She doesn't want to be the pretty possession of an older man who insists on controlling her. She refuses this glorified prostitution, the exchange of her body for diamonds and gold. I wonder if Sarah would have agreed with Simone de Beauvoir, who saw every marriage as a prostitution.

Sexual violence

There are several scenes in the film that hint at sexual violence, and, in particular, gang rape. Large, male hands catch Sarah's body as she falls down a shaft, and when she struggles to free herself, saying, "You're hurting me," they tell her that either she can let them touch her as they'd like or they can let her fall to her death. They call themselves Helping Hands and their voices tell us they are all male. She is subject to their will as they rush her into a decision: up or down? In another scene, Sarah walks alone in the woods but is suddenly surrounded by red, feathery demons called Fireys who call their posse the Fire Gang. The lyrics to their song go like this:

> We can show you a good time,
> And we don't charge nothin',
> Just strut your nasty stuff,
> Wiggle in the middle, yeah,
> Get the town talkin', fire gang.

These lyrics are ominous because they show that the members of the Fire Gang do not recognize themselves as dismemberers. Their own bodies are modular and break into smaller interchangeable units, but they fail to recognize that the bodies of others don't work the same way. They see themselves as mere enthusiasts of a good time, not as aggressors. Why doesn't Sarah just relax? What is her problem? Why is she so uptight about being beheaded? Why does she ruin their fun? The lyrics make clear, too, that sex is the subtext of it all. "Strut your nasty stuff," indeed.

They then assault her, trying to remove her head and dismember her. (There are obviously some racial implications in this scene—and several others in the film—but I'll leave that for a future essay.) Sarah tries to flee through the dark woods from this gang of devils who want to tear her apart.

Imposed motherhood

Her father and stepmother assume that Sarah will take on the role of surrogate mother when they're away. (In graduate school, I noticed that professors exclusively asked female stu-

dents, never male students, to babysit their children. Why?)
As a female, she is automatically seen as fit for the role and
is expected to put aside her plans to care for Toby. Motherhood comes first; all else, second. The only way Sarah could
possibly get out of babysitting would be, as her stepmother
explains, if she had plans to go on dates with boys. Dating
and courtship are the first steps toward motherhood and are
thus sanctioned by the family. However, her independent,
artistic endeavors—an interest in theater—are delegitimized
by the family structure, which needs her to perpetuate its
reproductive cycle. In early scenes in the film, it is sug-
gested that Sarah's mother died (there are newspaper clippings about her posted around Sarah's room, a private space
of womblike solace). There is only her wicked stepmother,
an archetype of many fairy tales; the genetic line with her
real mother has been ruptured. Female friendship or closeness is an impossibility in the film, confirming the cliché that
women are natural enemies to one another. A witchlike old
woman who calls her "dearie" tries to get her to accept a material life, to no avail. The matriarchs in the film are either
dead (Sarah's mother) or witchlike (the stepmother and the
garbage woman). So Sarah, like all girls, is conditioned to
have misgivings about what she must become: a mother. In
Western culture, becoming one's mother is the most hellish
of thoughts.

Doubt about the soundness of decisions made by women

She has learned not to trust her own intuitions. She seeks
advice from Hoggle, a coward, who tells her that his opinion
is superior to hers. The Helping Hands jeer at her decision to

go in the direction she was already headed: "She chose down?" they sneer. "Was that wrong?" she asks, second-guessing herself as everything in the scene suggests that she's made a poor choice. Threatening rocks with male faces and booming voices warn her not to go any farther, even though she is on the right path. Over and over, she is told to rethink what she has chosen, as though she is incapable of formulating a valid decision on her own. She seeks advice from a wise old man with a saucy bird on his head, a man who alternately calls her "young girl," "young woman," and "young lady." He offers counsel—a string of platitudes—and asks to be paid for his wisdom. Nearly every obstruction in the film takes a male form.

The obsession with beauty and femininity

In the opening scene, when Sarah practices for a play in the park, she wears jeans under her dress. This is a first sign of her resistance to the strictures of feminine beauty. Her stepmother wishes she would have dates with boys, insisting, "You *should* have dates at your age." Not going out makes Sarah freakish. Once inside her imaginary world, she tries to use her lipstick to draw orientation markers in the labyrinth, but these get manipulated by goblins, sending her in the wrong direction. Makeup throws everything off kilter, flipping values and making what was thought ugly into something seemingly beautiful. In the film, cosmetics equal deception. When Sarah loses her memory after eating the cursed peach, the little garbage lady tries to convince her that her life as a pretty young lady was what she was really looking for. She puts lipstick in her hand, which Sarah applies dreamily, unconvinced by its power. Two times in the film, Sarah breaks mirrors that show her beautiful, false images of herself. Women so often self-destruct because they are taught that their greatest enemy is looking at them through the mirror. (A tip: think of who profits from your not liking yourself and work actively to decrease those profits.) Sarah's approach is to destroy the ideal of feminine beauty that has deceived her, breaking it into powdery shards.

Old-fashioned etiquette toward women

Sir Didymus, the little dog who guards the bridge leading out of the Bog of Eternal Stench, is trained in the art of courtly manners. He treats Sarah like a proper lady, but his chivalrous behavior is laughable, with outsize courage for his miniature stature. Sarah short-circuits his valor through logic; he refuses to let her cross the bridge with her companions without his permission, so Sarah asks simply, "May we have your permission?" which disrupts his strict adherence to an irrelevant code. She is clearly capable of getting through the strange world with her own mind, without the aid of this small hero, whose self-importance nurses his myth of the helpless lady in distress. He is tiny because his world is far in the past, remote from us and thus perspectivally small.

Oblivion

Sarah ends up in the oubliette after she makes the decision to go down instead of up. As Hoggle tells her, the oubliette is where they put people so they can forget about them. Sarah is temporarily forced into a situation of obscurity. Like the many female artists, writers, thinkers, and musicians whose genius has been forgotten—dumped in the oubliette outside history, which is reserved primarily for men—Sarah escapes this oblivion with the help of Hoggle, who gives his reason for helping. He claims to dislike the thought of a "nice young girl" trapped in a "terrible black oubliette." In exchange for his help, she gives him a plastic bracelet. One could easily read in this exchange a similar dynamic between client and prostitute, the latter of whom gives an ersatz version of intimacy in exchange for her client's solicitousness. Sarah does what she needs to do to save herself from obscurity.

Time, the supposed enemy of women

She has only thirteen hours to get her half brother back. The clock presses on, accelerated at one point by the Goblin King after Sarah tells him the labyrinth is a piece of cake. In Western culture—and certainly elsewhere—women are made aware of their expiration date. If you aren't married by a certain age, you are doomed to a life of spinsterhood. Your biological clock ticks loudly and gives you a calendar by which to make the biggest decisions in your life. To frame it bluntly, Sarah must have the baby by the time the clock strikes. In their song "The Dangling Conversation," Simon and Garfunkel sing, "We note our place with bookmarkers that measure what we've lost." Time is what is lost, and for women, each wrinkle and grey hair represents a notch of bygone time like the bookmarks in the song. But Sarah beats the clock.

Feminine hygiene

The worst thing imaginable in the film is to smell bad. If one puts even a foot in the Bog of Eternal Stench, one will stink forever. Every girl knows, starting at the youngest age, that she has a duty to smell at all times like flowers and soap. Girls have to eliminate every smell that comes from their bodies—their sweat, their farts and shit, their vaginal secretions—lest they be judged undesirable. Sarah makes it safely through the Bog of Eternal Stench, defeating the stigma of feminine odor and the myth of the flawless and flowerlike female body.

Forced infantilization

Throughout the film, Sarah is urged over and over to remain a diminutive person, that is, a girl child. In the opening song, Bowie sings, "Don't tell me truth hurts, little girl," a first instance of infantilization of the protagonist. Everyone wants to freeze her in time as a pampered little girl. When she decides to take on the challenge of getting Toby back, the Goblin King urges, "Go back to your room. Play with your toys and your costumes." He does not want her in the wide-open civic space of adulthood. Our world is that of Nabokov's Humbert Humbert, who watches little girls play around him, suffering wistfully: "Ah, leave me alone in my pubescent park, in my mossy garden. Let them play around me forever. Never grow up." Sarah's room is a veritable dollhouse, full of cuddly miniatures that lull her into a nostalgic dreamscape of innocence and sweetness. As Susan Stewart has written in her beautiful book *On Longing: Narratives of the Miniature, the Gigantic, the Souvenir, the Collection*, the dollhouse holds a special place in the Western imagination:

> Occupying a space within an enclosed space, the dollhouse's aptest analogy is the locket or the secret recesses of the heart: center within center, within within within. The dollhouse is a materialized secret; what we look for is the dollhouse within the dollhouse and its promise of an infinitely profound interiority.

Girls are nothing but envelopes of secrets. They thrive in private and contain some inexplicable, hidden kernel of sweetness that everyone desires: "sugar and spice and everything nice." Something about their private, domestic, interior world resists the public space and keeps them from participating in it. Even as an adult, every woman is kept a child. When Sarah tries to join the bigger world—an imagined civic space, a kingdom of politics and power—trouble greets her. However, if she stays in her room—the space of feminine interiority, the womb—she is safe from responsibility as a sovereign subject. She bothers no one and no one bothers her. She is encouraged to stay a miniature princess in a glass coffin for all to see, like the music box she destroys by throwing it at the mirror. She was both Snow White and Sleeping Beauty, encased in a glass casket of dead beauty waiting for the lips of a prince. But she wakes up on her own and accepts her civic responsibility, entering the adult world with a defiant message to Jareth: "My will is as strong as yours, and my kingdom is as great."

The myth of privilege

As an American, Sarah is subject to a general sense of entitlement, which is a disservice to her. Throughout the film, as she encounters each new adversity, she shouts, "It's not fair!" At one point, the Goblin King retorts, "You say that so often. I wonder what your basis for comparison is." This is one of the few instances in which Jareth teaches Sarah a valuable lesson. As an American girl from a well-off family, she's never had to worry about anything. She is spoiled, living in a nice house with a room full of nice things. Her privileged living conditions make her apply her scale of values to the world at large, which skews her perspective. She expects things to be given to her, without needing to earn them. Until her adventure in the labyrinth, she lived under the American myth of entitlement. A pivotal moment arrives: Hoggle uses the "It's not fair!" line after Sarah steals his jewels, to which she replies, with a look of sudden comprehension in her face, "No, it isn't. But that's the way it is." She understands that unfairness is real, that no one is exempt from work or misfortune, and that her privilege is not guaranteed.

Consumerism

"It's all junk!": Sarah comes to this conclusion as the little old woman tries to make her forget that she was looking for Toby by leading her back to what appears to be her bedroom and thrusting material objects at her. The abundance of manufactured goods—toys, games, makeup—is not enough to keep Sarah from recognizing it all as distracting rubbish. The Goblin King's final entreaty to Sarah is the same one consumerist America makes to women—and everyone else—every day: "Look what I'm offering you. Your dreams. I ask for so little. Just let me rule you and you can have everything that you want. Just fear me, love me, do as I say, and I will be your slave." The Goblin King is a shape-shifter, able to transform himself into an owl, the symbol of wisdom. He can't get his way by using forthrightness, so he relies on deception. He makes crystal balls materialize from out of nowhere, miniature orbs onto which we project our desires. His crystalline screens show us the better version of ourselves we could be if we'd just surrender ourselves to him. But Sarah will have none of it. She jilts the American woman of the Guess Who's famous song: "Colored lights can hypnotize / sparkle someone else's eyes / American woman, stay away from me."

Labyrinth, as you can see, yields all the clues that help you to read it. Like Hansel and Gretel, the movie drops crumbs to show us the way.

I was in a coffee shop in New Haven and the barista told me she liked my hair. It is short and unruly and was particularly wind whipped on that day. We started talking about hair. She has short hair, too, and said it was a big change because she'd had very long hair her whole life. She said that at one point, her hair had been three feet long. A former Rapunzel was making me my drink. She had decided on a whim to hatchet it all off. She told me about an episode of the cartoon *Adventure Time* called "To Cut a Woman's Hair," in which the protagonist Finn has to get a lock of princess hair for a balding witch who wants to be beautiful. After the quest fails, he tries a different approach. He says to her, "Having beautiful hair isn't going to get you anywhere, because you're ugly inside and out." Ruefully, the witch explains, "I thought if I had some beautiful hair, I could learn to love myself." Finn reveals that under his hat, he has long flowing locks of hair, which he offers to the witch in lieu of princess hair. The barista said she found the cartoon's emphasis on women's hair very remarkable, the sign of a larger cultural problem that is particularly obvious to us now, with the renewed fashion of long-tressed women in commercials and in the street, still trying to have princess hair despite the silliness of the idea. I told her I'd always found it strange that men gain power with their hair (think of the luscious locks of metal dudes or Jesus) and that having their hair cut is a symbolic castration (remember the Samson and Delilah story). On the contrary, women gain power when they cut their hair. Often, after leaving a boyfriend or girlfriend, women cut off their hair as a sign of empowerment and freedom. There is something awesome about running clippers across your scalp and watching a story you're tired of fall to the floor. I asked the barista if she felt relieved to be free of all that weight when she cut off her pounds of hair. For a woman to cut off her hair is to dump the dead weight of someone else's ideal. After I told her my ideas about hair and power, I asked her if she remembered the line from *Labyrinth*, "You have no power over me." She smiled and said, "That just gave me chills."

All cultural artifacts may be read like *Labyrinth*. They each contain hidden meanings, hidden even from their creators. The collective subconscious has a way of surfacing in all the things we make. "You have no power over me" is not just for women. It is for anyone who has ever lost to the Man; that is to say, everybody. Including the Man himself.

The Bad Serious

The word "gravity" has two meanings. It is no coincidence that we associate seriousness with heaviness. In Milan Kundera's novel *The Unbearable Lightness of Being* (1984), the protagonist Tomas lingers between two choices: a heavy life or a light one. The heavy life involves fidelity and the weighed-down but substantial realness of shared living, while the light life involves infidelity and ungrounded, disorienting freedom. This double vision unfolds throughout the novel's pages as Tomas toggles back and forth between a light life and a heavy one, weighing the virtues and defects of each. The themes in Kundera's book are of no less importance today than they were in 1984. I started first grade that year as a six-year-old already demonstrating a tendency toward psychological heaviness. Each night before I fell asleep, I would imagine, in a terrifying enumeration, what would happen if each of my family members died. It was a kind of addiction to sadness. I wasn't such a melancholic kid, but my hypothetical mind always drifted toward the worst-case scenario, perhaps because of the Red Scare atmosphere in the air, which asked us all to imagine the coming nuclear cataclysm. The fear seems silly now. Quite a few of my Russian friends have told me they were just as scared of us when they were kids. I've lost my Russophobia, even in the midst of the Russian encroachments in Ukraine happening as I write this sentence. Lesson learned early on: people are not their governments. Rarely are we ever truly represented by them.

The questions Kundera posed back in 1984 are impressively relevant today. While his apparent focus was the problem of fidelity or infidelity, one can extrapolate from his book a much broader set of questions about how to live. Without recognizing it consciously, each one of us decides every single day whether we'd prefer a light life or a heavy one. Most of us try out both at some point and then ultimately pick one or the other for the big things (jobs, relationships, spiritual life, etc.), committing to a life of stability or a life of mutability. For the small stuff, a patchwork of light and heavy habits makes up our existential quilt. This is the central concern of politics: to sway us toward a light or a heavy life, to turn the individual's problem into a collective one. Since 1984, we've developed many new debates on heaviness and lightness, sometimes in a literal form—the politics of weight loss or anorexia—but more often in a figurative form: debates about polyamory, who can marry whom, and other civic questions about fidelity and couplehood; the lightness of new media and the disposability of our products; and the loosening and implicit lightening of moral values. While doing research for one of his novels, the French writer Michel Tournier visited garbage dumps all over the world and made an interesting observation: the trash of poor people is heavy and the trash of wealthy people is light. Why? Because when you are desperately poor, you use and reuse what you have—like plastic sacks and bottles and boxes—leaving only the heavy organic remains of apple cores, chicken bones, and potato peels to slump in the folds of the trash bag. On the other hand, the wealthy not only buy more; what they buy is swaddled in superfluous cardboard and cellophane. They are caught in a diaphanous and disposable dream, wafting upward like a Louis Vuitton receipt caught in the wind.

The typical American (is there such a thing?) would probably opt for lightness given the choice. This contemporary attraction to the weightless takes a digital form or manifests itself in endless televised dreams of freeing oneself from the cumbersome anchors of family, work, aging, and heaviness in whatever shape. The principle is to stay buoyant, bobbing atop the crests of waves, saving the depths till after death. Lightness is for many the highest of virtues, as it seems to resist the downward pull of mortality. Staying up above it, looking down at the plebeians from the lofty confines of your loft apartment or from the womblike solace of your SUV; or better yet, digitizing your whole person, a guarantee of eternal and weightless life: these airy escapes lift us from the fact of our impermanence. Freedom narratives—*On the Road, Easy Rider, Into the Wild*—always sell well because they allow for a vicarious appropriation of liberty, consumed even from the confines of a cubicle, a jail cell, or some other space of detention. I suspect that much of the lightness that makes up contemporary life is part of a trompe l'oeil fresco meant to distract from heavier matters. Debbie Downer has been gagged. The wet blanket has been tossed in the dryer with a fragrant and feather-thin Downy Simple Pleasures dryer sheet.

There is no lack of serious faces today. They generally serve as frontispieces for hermetically sealed minds, books shut so tight they can never be opened. Those with serious faces believe in fundaments and foundations; each of their thoughts and words is mobilized in the name of truth. They are happy to die for their creed, to torch the holy books and tenets of others, to splash hate about on the Internet; they relish the decimation of difference. But if you made an island just for these serious-faced types, handpicked from their communities across the planet, this self-wrecking population would implode faster than the four-minute duration of Megadeth's "Symphony of Destruction," a fitting sound track for the ensuing bloodbath.

A man announces in all seriousness that the apocalypse is near. People perk up, receptive to his message. They've seen the signs, too. When you've convinced yourself of the nearness of the end, everything becomes a sign that confirms its imminence. Middle East chaos, the death of millions of bees, school shooting sprees, the collapse of morality, weird weather, the gays getting married, the marijuanification of the U.S.: all omens of impending doom. Pray a lot and arm yourself. Build a bunker, invest in gold. Print a gun on your 3-D printer so the government won't know it exists and thus can't take it away from you. Live like a clenched fist. Punch at the specters.

If there really is an end on the horizon, it will be brought about by the same paranoiacs who imagine it. Aesop's fable about the oak that fell because it was too unyielding in the wind, in contrast to the reed that bends in the breeze, is still relevant. The moral: bend rather than break. The kind of alarmism we see now always existed but is made worse by the many new ways to broadcast it. The "what ifs" loom and urge us to buy safety. The selling voice speaks with urgency in a grave tone. We could use far less of this kind of seriousness.

When the model snipes us with that serious gaze from the catwalk or from the pages of a magazine, what does she want to tell us? (We will say "she" because this is what she usually is.) Why can she not smile? What has foreclosed her joy? The model knows things we will never know. She is serious because she has gotten a glimpse behind the scenes of the system. She knows that her body must resemble a coat hanger in its slightness and neutrality. The clothes should drape on her non-body as if suspended from a clothesline. She isn't intended to fill them in, only to make them move in three-dimensional space. A smile is not neutral, and it is thus forbidden. She is made relentlessly aware of her shelf life. She knows she is all lightness—she has no weight, no duration, will leave no lasting impression—which is the heaviest of feelings. Remember this the next time you see her, caught at the crease in the slim pages of *Vogue*.

The unattentive person might read her gaze as a look of desire. But desire is a signature of vitality, of which she has little. The image world is uninterested in intimacy and sensuality except as signs; there, her body is only useful as a giving sign, not as a recipient of pleasure. Her job, rather, is to imitate the same lifelessness of the garment products she exhibits. Fashion Week, each day of which is a Día de las Muertas, brings the skeletal parade to the couture capitals of the world. High heels tap out the rhythms of a funerary march, low and subtly thunderous in unison, a *basso continuo* under the cold electronic beats of a hired DJ. Again, we could use far less of this kind of seriousness.

Tatyana Fazlalizadeh's street art project *Stop Telling Women to Smile* addresses a real problem: when women walk down the street, men they don't know will often tell them to smile. This ice-breaking flirtation tries to get the woman's attention, to make her feel pretty, and to turn her into the sweet, vulnerable, attention-seeking darling she's meant to be. What at first seems a harmless gesture proves to be a general incapacity to deal with a woman who doesn't make the effort to be pleasing. I've been solicited to smile throughout the U.S. and Europe by complete strangers. While I do have acute Southern Smile Syndrome around people I know, my face is sober when I walk alone because I'm thinking. Always in my head when wandering through cities, I like to maintain the requisite pensive solemnity these thoughts need to swell. I'm not sad. I'm not depressed. I'm not angry. I'm in the process of birthing an awesome idea. And my labor shouldn't be disturbed by somebody's generic solicitation. I already saw you there, probably long before you saw me (we are wary by necessity), and if I wanted to smile at you, I already would have. His Coy Mistress is not coy; she's just not interested.

Perhaps this is what the model's serious gaze is supposed

to imitate: the eternal woman who passes you by, never returning your gaze, never reciprocating your smile, driving you mad with longing. The catwalk is a staged street scene of drop-dead passersby oblivious to your existence. The eternal return of the girl from Ipanema who "just doesn't see," over and over on the platform, passing you by without even a nuance of recognition. You buy what she wears, either to take on some of her majestic indifference or to have a remnant of the one who left you invisible.

Increasing numbers of serious people are cropping up and pooling their energies. They want to inflict their own pain on everyone else. They type quickly, letters spraying like machine-gun shells, filling the Internet with bullet holes. Their smile only surfaces in response to the ugly ideas they've crafted. Their relationship with the world is punitive. They fill radio with hate transmissions, airwaves that sizzle like quivering oil on a too-hot griddle. They see the world through fun-house mirrors, which distort big into small and small into big. Grinches and stooges in basements; trolls with golden microphones, head veins throbbing; salt-and-pepper all-American haircut, tailored suit, generous sponsors, and lots of pent-up aggression. They try to be the dead weight that pulls everyone else down with them. So many new brands of solemnity. A panoply of sournesses and acidities to choose from. A Molotov cocktail concocted mostly from bitters.

It is conceivable that very serious people have shorter lives than everyone else. I've met a few individuals whose faces I cannot even picture smiling. Their resentment is so palpable, one can sense it in the dark. Their sky is always falling. They imagine life as a long string of catastrophes in the form of potholes, trip wires, bear traps, IEDs, speed bumps, cliff edges, swamps, mines, barbed-wire fences, booby traps, moats, and quicksand. The default assumption is that everyone around is a potential enemy. Even friends are capable of inflicting pain. The defensive soul wears a ballistic vest whenever it meets others. A piece of shrapnel from some painful event long ago has lodged itself in their person and just festers there, underneath layers and layers of Kevlar. Why do so many wounded and serious souls dwell in America today? Why such pressing gloom? Why this pattern of confrontational seriousness? The serious soul is doubtless haunted by some repressed inner demon whose choke hold cannot be loosened, but one wonders: is there any iteration of seriousness that is not bound up in tropes of closed-mindedness, dour-faced severity, and heaviness? Is there some *other kind of serious*?

The Other Serious

In the end, we are always rewarded for our good will, our patience, fair-mindedness, and gentleness with what is strange.

—FRIEDRICH NIETZSCHE, *The Gay Science*

For whatever reason, the present always feels unprecedented. It isn't. Because we rarely recognize the patterns of the past, which recycle themselves endlessly, we have a constant sense of braving the unknown. But the unknown is just the known in disguise. In his book *This Compost*, whose title comes from a poem by Walt Whitman, Jed Rasula unearthed a recurring trope in American poetry: the idea of culture transmission as a kind of composting process. Ideas die and decompose in the earth. They are taken up in new moments, having been reconfigured by subterranean processes, unrecognizable in their new forms. The earth gives itself back to itself, through itself. The worm, an ugly thing, is a maker of the new. It processes fallen scraps of life and sends them off living again through the roots of plants, which feed everything else. An enchanting thought: ideas are up-cycled by time through an abject reworking of their structure, rendering them unfamiliar to us. The corpse becomes flower. The uncanny is just an improbable recognition that occurs when we are faced with this reshaped thing.

It is due time for a different kind of serious, newly processed into something we barely recognize: an Other Serious.

Calling for seriousness in our ludic moment is a risk. Even suggesting such a thing leads to accusations of dogmatism. Through the examples of the Bad Serious I've given, like apocalypse fetishists and joyless ideologues, we get a cursory understanding of what *not* to be. If this is how the serious behave, why would anyone ever want to be serious? Who could blame the ironic masses for fleeing to the remote end of the expressive spectrum to be as far away as possible from this kind of bad faith, fear, and cynicism? I want to understand what has forced half the population into an unbearably heavy seriousness and the other half into an unbearably light, confettilike eruption of irony. These two dominant tendencies suck all the color out of the expressive spectrum. We are due for a consequential, polychromatic expansion of forms that will add new hues to our communicative palette. I'm not sure if we can describe the Other Serious as translucent, a shallow synthesis of solemnity and irony. I'd like to think of it as something other than a simple merging of two old enemy concepts. Rather, it accumulates ways to make humans feel human again, not relying on the patterns that made us lose our humanity in the first place. It is not a simple third option; it is a precondition for the proliferation of innumerable options.

What place is there today for a young and contemplative person who doesn't feel like guffawing at stupid jokes or living as a human barometer of trends and silly trivia? Is it possible to be twenty and committed to reading and thinking without apologizing for it by calling oneself a nerd? Seriousness has gotten a bad name, reduced to a crude parody of itself and devoid of the richness that should be part of any mode of human expression. History is full of serious types: Hitlers, Stalins, Mussolinis, Gaddafis, bin Ladens, Westboro Baptists, corporate moguls, self-convinced academics, apologists of orthodoxy, precipitants of the apocalypse, and various and sundry ideologues. In a few contexts, to call someone serious is still a compliment, but by and large, the word is negatively connoted in the U.S. It is something to be left to the Europeans. "Why are you so serious?": the eternal question posed to someone who is not smiling quite enough. If you are reading quietly, thinking deeply, not grinning and saying bubbly things, you might just be a burgeoning bin Laden. Do people fear that the unsmiling person is at risk of tipping over into full-on Stalinism?

If there has been a surge among young people to embrace religion again, which seemed to be fading back in the '90s, I believe it has less to do with a new spiritual zeal and more to do with the solemn grounding that religion offers. In the best case, religion asks you to take interest in a text, to spend a lot of quiet time with it and to do a lot of thought work (prayer), to think in terms of community, to let your life be guided by a set of principles, and to think holistically about living. The secular age did not fill the void left by religion with something else, and this is why many are turning back to faith, or at least to the model of living it offers. In part, the current appeal of religion is its monastic form and the natural community it engenders. While some people are very capable of finding reasons on their own to be good, thoughtful, and engaged in the world, many clearly need an external structure to give form to their actions. There is an incipient, collective loneliness caused in part by digital communication, which isolates people and gives fewer and fewer reasons for really digging life. The Web is a junkscape; while an occasional treasure can be found, you're mostly wading through detritus. If you are a conscious modern soul who feeds off the Internet, you suspect that your distraction-filled hours will have piled up into what will equal little more than meager survival. Religion at least offers a structure for organizing these accumulated hours. The holy day—Saturday or Sunday or Wednesday or whenever—is a standing appointment with God. It's something to be counted on. And you know when you arrive at your place of worship, you'll be greeted by people who are on their best behavior and who want to join with you for a couple of hours to try and make the world meaningful in a serious way. How do people, aware of the inherent contradictions of religion, reconcile their hesitations about the doctrine with the need for a welcoming and serious environment like this one? It is surprising that a widespread effort to make a secular version of the temple/mosque/synagogue/church has not been successful. In some ways, the university resembles this, with people meeting at regular times to read and discuss issues that interest them, but the format of most classes does not allow for much intimacy, and once you graduate, the congregation ends. The workplace is the closest thing some people have to a stable community with a serious atmosphere, although there have been many efforts to remove seriousness from the office as well. You can join a book club, a sports team, or a cooking class, but these are interest-based gatherings and don't really answer any big questions. What is the alternative?

We live in a world of undecidability, a world with lots of grey areas and striated spaces, always in flux, changing with each new element that is added or taken away. While a first reactionary impulse might be either to get serious about forcing the world to make sense or to make a big joke out of the whole thing, I am in favor of a spirit that Keats called "negative capability," a characteristic possessed by someone who is "capable of being in uncertainties, mysteries, doubts without any irritable reaching after fact and reason." What bothers us so much about not knowing? We consistently invent provisional truths and impose them on everyone else, or, when we acknowledge how truths crumble, we turn sarcastic toward anyone dumb enough to believe in something. It is possible, and perhaps necessary, to keep these tendencies in check. By refusing to rely on a closed set of tenets or to take everything as just another occasion for unrestrained mockery, one is less likely to foreclose the generous possibilities existence offers. There have been attempts to halt the destructive cycle. For example, sincerity has been proposed as an antidote to the pervasive irony of our moment. The dichotomy of irony versus sincerity is clean and predictable, a perfectly reasonable binary. And while I would certainly be on board for a sincere overhaul of the irony machine, it seems to me that what is missing even more than forthrightness is a solemn profundity not bound by ideology. Sincerity—or a closely related word, authenticity—is difficult to evaluate because it involves the subjective judgment of a person's intentions, words, or presence. Sincerity is more a social than a personal phenomenon. (It is possible to be insincere with yourself—i.e., through bad faith—but this is a special kind of pathology.) Seriousness, on the other hand, pertains both to the individual and the collective, to the inside and the outside at the same time. It describes the way something is done or thought and can be recognized externally. I get the sense that people are ready to be serious, but the only seriousness available is currently wielded by the uncool. "Uncool" here doesn't mean "unhip"; I mean that these serious types are too fiery in temperament. In contemporary America, our convection is all off. A certain coolness can be of help in getting by in our world, one that lets the thermal molecules of consciousness move more slowly, in bluish arcs. This is why I want to propose what I call the Other Serious as an alternative to the destructive kind of solemnity and to the helpless ironization of everything, those two poles, somehow both thermally frantic, that seem to characterize our moment. Let's think through this Other Serious in pieces, giving a name to its characteristics and cobbling together what it might look like pragmatically.

1. The Other Serious is calm

You have likely noticed the surge of vitriol, especially in politics, that keeps us perpetually keyed up. What are we supposed to do with all of this choleric exuberance, even if we recognize it as a staged anger play meant to turn us into a riled-up and vulnerable audience, all for the sake of increasing someone's profit margin? Starting a public conversation is an invitation to a flame war. Regardless of what you say, someone will insult you very loudly in all caps with almost comical indignation. I say almost comical because, while these folks resemble petulant children in their melodramatic outpourings, they're sometimes successful in steering the conversation in their direction. The voice of the calm person is less entertaining than the voice of the shrieking reactionary. Imagine for a moment that you are the sum of your tweets. For many of us, this will be the digital residue left after we're dead: comments, reviews, opinions, and ratings left behind in the cracks of the Internet. You get a lot about a person's character, a near-perfect picture of their insecurities and shortcomings, by adding this stuff up. The irascible person sticks out like a sore thumb. At no time in history have people been so eager to publicize their own soreness. Calm and measured people somehow maintain a buffer between their thoughts and the world. Less apt to take things personally, the calm person listens, thinks, and answers. They recognize the weakness veiled by people's insults and they respond as one should to a weak person. This kind of serious equanimity aids in the unsimmering of a culture at its boiling point.

The coolness involved in the Other Serious does not involve a cold-heartedness, just a cool-heartedness. The strongest form of love is the one whose heat has subsided some. The early hotness of all passions is the result of those fleshy glands that shoot their stuff into our bloodstreams. The body and mind are volatile when they give themselves over to heat.

Because fever can't be argued with, the hotheaded are always put in the position of needing to apologize for mistakes they made when they were flushed. But cool-hearted people can declare their love with conviction, not needing to spend a good part of life going back to correct the aftermath of their impulses. Cool-hearted love is not lesser love; on the contrary, it is the most durable kind of love.

A temporal component is involved in the slow patience of the Other Serious, which gets to things in unhurried time. Thoughts of any depth require a purposeful duration for the brainwork to happen. Nietzsche speaks again: "Lightning and thunder require time, the light of the stars requires time, deeds require time even after they are done, before they can be seen and heard." Our collective chrono-philosophy, the attitude toward time that guides shared life these days, is a quick, slipshod time that rushes past inconvenient thoughts, uncomfortable facts, and beautifully sluggish realities, always looking toward what is about to arrive. An alternative to this sprint past the now and on to more thrilling tomorrows could take shape as a steady and quiet accumulation of experience and a depressurized assimilation of old and new ideas. In the spirit of the Other Serious, we could grant time to things that require it unconditionally and that, as of late, have been neglected, whipped about in the tailwinds of hurried people. To remain temporally calm is to disregard the will to hustle and, instead, to step out of this relentless flow and resist what has become the default treatment of time. The Other Serious is monastic in form but not in content. Its clock runs at the pace of a sundial in a cloister garden. It involves a practice of reading and concentration, of time spent above the weak concepts that tend to govern us now.

2. The Other Serious is middle seeking

One of its primary principles is to resist polarities. The idea is to assemble a collective that transcends the tired categories of nation, age, race, gender, and creed. Have we not in some sense outgrown these old classifications and hackneyed conflicts? How much time and energy—and, in the worst case, blood—do we waste when we accept our role as inheritors of someone else's age-old insecurities and aggressions, someone else's superiority or inferiority complexes, someone else's role as oppressor or victim? If everyone is bent on settling the score and convinced that their inherited worldview is the only one that really counts, lacking the imagination to realize that a person who grew up half a world away is just as firmly convinced about their set of truths—no less inherited than our own—we'll be living and dying in another very long and sour century. We are not mere bodily containers of our ancestors' prejudices. We have no contract with them. We are not obliged to take up where they left off, like characters in an Émile Zola novel, destined for a genetically determined life of toxic habits and unreflective automaticity, the mere unfolding of a hereditary experiment in this laboratory called life. Marks are left on us all by things that happened long before our births and by the conditions under which we make our entrance on this planet, but we do have some measure of say in what we will make of these inherited birthmarks. As the thirteenth-century Persian poet and mystic Rumi counseled, "Be melting snow. Wash yourself of yourself." There are many ways to read this dictum, one of which is this: by washing yourself of all that was conferred on you by your circumstances and by rinsing away the ego that came with this conferral, you dissolve and fuse with something bigger than yourself. Remaining intact as snow, you stay cold and you go nowhere. If you melt from ice cold to cool, you travel beyond what you know and what you were given and you feed something beyond your own personhood. You develop a molecular consciousness that tunes in with that of others who've melted. I am a fact, you are a fact, and in our blended facticity, we can shape the conversation as we like it. Recognize in others what they did and did not choose. The Other Serious thinks past bequeathed binaries; it works as a bridge between so-called high and low culture, between the known and the unknown, between the now and the not now. Those engaged in its conscious application can look at their own milieu from outside it, to estrange their habitual way of looking. In short, the Other Serious refuses the separation between "this" and "that." Both a hovering over the panorama of life and an immersive plunge in experience, the Other Serious has the power to connect international pools of responsive and mindful people. It has living eyes and looks across the planet, in the crannies and nooks of culture, to find ideas sympathetic to it.

Because the world tends to experience itself more and more through media, it is also imperative to create a space of resistance against this current. The lucid patterns of the Other Serious lead the brain away from the deadening effects of mediatized life. This does not necessarily entail a total refusal of media; it simply calls media out on its propensity to overreach. The Other Serious announces to all media: "You are in my personal space. Kindly take a step back." At arm's length, media is more easily scrutinized and less inclined to encroach on human sovereignty. It is difficult to study a whole whale if you are trapped inside its belly; for all of you who are in your twenties and younger, you were actually born inside. You thus experience it more viscerally than those of us who watched it swim up. Again, this is an example of the middle-seeking drive of the Other Serious, as it doesn't call for a total repudiation of media, just a cool detachment from it.

The Other Serious is intellectually agnostic; it doesn't commit to a particular school of thought or to some specific method. It borrows at will from various philosophical strands or literary or artistic movements or epistemological modes and benefits from the reconfiguration of what is already there, all the while welcoming new things that arrive in time.

3. The Other Serious is attentive

To pay attention is to stretch the mind and the eyes toward an object, as is implicit in the word's Latin root *tendere*, to stretch. There is a reason why metaphors of cognition so often involve a physical analogue. Because thought is abstract, it is more easily metaphorizable, and because the brain is housed in the body, this is a handy place to find in one of its gestures a figure for talking about that grey matter that governs it. Mind and body are at least contiguous, if not mutually suffused. Take the word "comprehend," for example. It shares the same root as the word "prehensile," as in prehensile tail, a tail that can grab things. The mind becomes a hand; to comprehend is to clutch knowledge and to pay attention is to hold a thought with this same cerebral hand. Thought is imagined as a manual, almost tentacular operation, the hands replacing the eyes and brain as foraging mechanisms. Verbs of cognition are amazing places to look for the forgotten metaphors that made them possible. "To ruminate" is to chew cud, like a cow. "To ponder" is to weigh, from the same root as the unit of measure, the pound. "To contemplate" meant to mark out a space for observation, just like the augur, the religious official in ancient Rome who tried to read signs; the words "temple" and "template" share this same root. "To consider" has an unclear etymology, but seems to be linked to the stars, the same root as "sidereal." "To muse" is to stick one's nose or muzzle in the air. "To brood" is to incubate or hatch by warmth. "To conjecture" means to throw together, with the same root as "object," "inject," and "reject." In short, all of these latent meanings I was able to compile with just a little attention to language, that omnipresent, communicative matter that inflects our every thought and action.

You can never focus your attention on language enough, nor can you observe and read enough. This fact is not disheartening; it is thrilling. The infinity of the task means an infinity of purpose. From attention to the smallest aesthetic detail to the most panoramic kind of attention, focus affords us the opportunity to gather our faculties around a single fire. I'm referring, in a final etymological intimation, to the forgotten meaning of "focus," the fire or the hearth, a warm gathering place, a point of convergence around a point of light. This is what Other Serious attention is: the multiplication of these points of light toward which we turn our consciousness.

4. The Other Serious is improvisational

Through the optic of the Other Serious, you choose your object of focus and let your mind get improvisational with it. Each thought is a deliberate undermining of reflexes and assumptions. Stare at any word long enough and you revive it. Stare at the features of the building in which you live and its architecture looks back at you. Turn your process of looking into a structured chaos—humble in nature, small in scope—that gives form to thought and that does not panic when faced with the unknown. The world is your snow globe; you delight in shaking it up.

One place where I've seen the kind of serious improvisation I mean is a well-known Web site called Rookie. It is ostensibly a feminist site for high school–age girls, but its open attitude has earned it a much broader audience. What's best about the site is the way it disregards all that is divisive, focusing instead on what is possible rather than what isn't. The site has become more or less an improvisational space for young women to try out various modes of expression, in a kind of creative echo chamber for philosophical, literary, musical, and artistic spontaneity, closed only to hater culture. In other words, it supports the proliferation of new or reconfigured forms and thus disregards the blockades that arise through our hostile online culture of anonymous criticism and brainless commentary. Rookie somehow neutralizes the domineering and contrarian voice and replaces it with a polyvocal consent, a collective voice of approbation for the trying out of new ideas.

5. The Other Serious is curatorial

What I mean here is that each gesture of the Other Serious is infused with care. The words "caring" and "careful" are insufficient in describing precisely what I mean, the first because it has parental or sentimental connotations and the second because it has connotations of vigilance and prudence, a kind of existential frugality. By care, I mean a total self-investment in the thing at hand, a carving out of some unit of significance between yourself and whatever you may be contemplating. The French philosophers Gilles Deleuze and Félix Guattari used a memorable image to describe how things may set up relationships between themselves, what they called a process of deterritorialization and reterritorialization. The unit they imagined was formed by a wasp and an orchid, which enter into a reciprocal relationship with each other, the orchid in some sense becoming wasplike and the wasp taking on something of the orchid in its being. Martin Buber, the Austrian-born Israeli philosopher, created a similar analogy in his description of the experience of contemplating a tree. He writes:

> [I]t can also happen, if will and grace are joined, that as I contemplate the tree I am drawn into a relation, and the tree ceases to be an It. [. . .] The tree is no impression, no play of my imagination, no aspect of a mood; it confronts me bodily and has to deal with me as I must deal with it—only differently.

To be concerned with the object at hand is to *co-mingle* and enter into a self-implicated proximity with it. We might think of this relationship as a kind of curation. The job of the curator is different from that of the caregiver. While both involve a stewardship and the preservation of something precious that might be lost otherwise—art or life—the curator's vocation involves an aesthetic proficiency and an accumulation of many modes of looking. The curator is responsible for a heritage, for answering the question, "What is meaningful about this picture?" and for contextualizing a singular object in a vast history and a potentially planet-wide geography. The curator is the embodiment of interdisciplinarity; she must think simultaneously about aesthetics, history, logistics, and finances; she has to think about the materiality of the object and its abstract implications; she has to put herself in the place of the spectator and try to imagine the experience of moving through an exhibition, an almost empathic responsibility; and all of this is done with care.

6. The Other Serious is joyful

The most important aspect of the Other Serious is its smile. It cannot scowl or pout. It carries no billy club or pepper spray, only a book of questions. It is fueled by joy and focus; its emissions are low-volume jubilation and the desire to keep on looking. There is an important antecedent to this joyful seriousness in philosophy, what Nietzsche calls *gay science*. (The extent to which Nietzsche has imposed his presence in this essay is both startling and delightful to me.) In his *On the Genealogy of Morals*, he describes it this way:

> [T]here seems to be nothing *more* worth taking seriously [than the problems of morality], among the rewards for it being that someday one will perhaps be allowed to take them *cheerfully*. For cheerfulness—or in my own language *gay science*—is a reward: the reward of a long,

brave, industrious, and subterranean seriousness, of which, to be sure, not everyone is capable.

Nietzsche took the expression "gay science" from the Provençal expression *gaia scienza* or *gai saber*, which is what he calls in *Ecce Homo* "that unity of *singer, knight*, and *free spirit* which distinguishes the wonderful early culture of the Provençals from all equivocal cultures." (He's referring to the troubadour-inspired poets of the fourteenth century.) In a spirit reminiscent of Nietzsche's cheerful seriousness, the Other Serious is malleable, open equally to science and poetry, open to everything and its opposite. It is simultaneously effusive and contained; its joy goes right up to the brim. While there exists a vast taxonomy of smiles in human social commerce, the one that best matches the Other Serious is an internal one, one that has virtually nothing to do with the mouth but rather with something we might call the *esprit*, which can be translated as "spirit" or "intellect." It is a smile that belongs to you, that warms subtly from the inside out, a barely incandescent mound of embers that feed themselves.

These six characteristics give form to a kind of seriousness no less committed in its taking account of the world but free of the ideological obstinacy that typifies the dominant seriousness of the now. I wrote this piece with a specific group of people in mind, namely, people in their teens, twenties, and thirties who are left unsatisfied by the communicative habits most prevalent today. Habits are made to be broken. A simple consciousness, not just of *what* you think but also of *the attitude through which* you think it, can begin to enrich an otherwise impoverished range of expression. While there are certainly cases when you should be content to quietly accept what you're given, this is not one of them. There are options besides ironic dissimulation, oppressive seriousness, and absolute silence. A bit of composure—emptied of sarcasm and bad faith, emptied of a reactionary or even punitive impulse—brings with it just enough weight and self-possession to make a ground from which thought can depart without floating away into nothing.

Recently, a friend and I organized a sing-along evening. People arrived with food and drinks and we gathered around my old Yamaha keyboard and we sang some songs. I can play decent chords, so I hammered away on the faux ivories while everyone sang in unison to the Beatles and such. After the first song, no one seemed self-conscious. We were all a little out of tune, a little off rhythm, a little sketchy on the lyrics, and in our numinous imperfection, we made what turned out to be an intimate evening with a real sense of camaraderie. You should have seen it. We projected the song lyrics onto a wall and everyone sat around on the floor or near the keyboard, drinks in hand, faces glowing a little from the wine and the projector beam. It was no Dionysian orgy, no photo op to be splashed all over Facebook to corroborate that fun had been had. It was just an honest evening. People passed around a guitar; they made spirited requests; they stepped out for a cigarette.

Those in attendance were mostly German and American grad students who'd perhaps sung a little karaoke in their lives, but who'd not yet enjoyed the kumbaya excellence of the sing-along tradition. I organized one of these things in Paris once, in the basement of a fancy university where an old, out-of-tune piano sat amid vintage fencing equipment. My buddy brought his guitar and all of us sang and played and drank. We were all foreign students, a little lonesome in cheerless Paris, and we fought off the blues by singing the blues. We'd found a low-cost, inclusive way to spend meaningful time with one another and we weren't in a church. There was nothing resembling a dogma in the vicinity. I think this kind of gathering could serve as a model for serious and secular intimacy. While singing doesn't allow for much conversation, it does generate closeness and an intense kind of focus. As we sang, no one at our recent sing-along was bothered by upcoming prospectus defenses, the courses to be taught the next morning, or the abysmal job market. We steered the evening, with joy as our copilot. We were just there, together, clustered around a common task: trying to produce a recognizable tune. I'm too young to be an old hippie, but I can understand why gatherings in those psychedelic days were most often organized around music. There's something unifying about these squiggly waves that vibrate the eardrums. Committing one's life to the making or study of music, art, literature, or contemplative thought has the feel of a real vocation. This serious self-application to an infinite task—none of these are finishable endeavors—means you are fueling your own contentment and potentially creating the conditions for the contentment of others. My keyboard skills are weak compared to trained musicians, but I don't fret about it: they were good enough to make a nice evening among friends. With more rigorous practice, one could multiply these evenings and polish their edges, a self-perpetuating motive to keep going. Even as a hobby, working hard at music, art, or other expressive enterprises is one of the signatures of a worthwhile life. I know so many people who listened to tons of new music in high school, who filled sketchbooks with drawings, who wrote little poems in private. As grown-ups, they've abandoned all of that essential stuff to watch TV instead. They're too tired to dig for new songs. There's something too bittersweet about pulling out the old sketchbook. They think their old poems were dumb. But, friends, when you're dead, what's left of you? I wish I had silly sketches from my great-grandparents or recordings of their voices. Maybe they spent their whole lives working away at their jobs, but I have no proof of it. These little things—jotted-down thoughts and memories of good deeds or pain, rudimentary melodies recorded in spite of bad acoustics—these are the things left behind in your existential wake. A thought that is never written down or acted upon might as well have never been thought. Time well spent is time dedicated to leaving a record of your acquaintance with our humble home in orbit. Do a favor for your future elderly self: make cool things you can dig out of a box and say, "I made this." Prove to the geriatric you that you spent your hours well.

That covers time, but what about space? There is a way to make one's space conducive to deep thinking. You don't necessarily have to throw your TV into the dumpster; you can donate it or sell it on Craigslist. The Spanish Surrealist Salvador Dalí wrote *50 Secrets of Magic Craftsmanship*, an astounding book that seems at first to be about the secrets of painting but that turns out to be a blueprint for a different way to live. He converts the world into a walk-in studio where strange things are always afoot. He tells how to build an aranearium, a structure that invites spiders to build their webs inside it, thus feeding the artist's visions. The residence has the potential to foster the good kind of seriousness. Architecture and the arrangement of space could solve many existential problems by creating atmospheres amenable to serious brainwork and conviviality. A former professor of mine thinks that every university should sponsor a twenty-four-hour, on-campus coffee shop (in his vision, it is smoker friendly) with books lying around, where people can gather at all hours and talk about ideas. Nocturnal thinking is in many ways more intense than diurnal thinking, allowing for the conscious and the subconscious to converge. I think what bothers him about the contemporary university is a very conspicuous fact, which I experienced again ten minutes ago, a repetition of something that happens each day on campuses all across the States.

I was taking a snack break at a university café, eavesdropping as usual, and confirmed once again that students don't talk about ideas; they talk about logistics and bureaucracy. They talk about papers (not the topics of these papers, but the quantity of them still left to hand in) and problem sets and due dates and labs and grades and internships and the administrative details of study abroad. I hear lots of numbers: how many hours they slept, how many points they need for an A, how many appointments they have before Friday. They never seem to talk about *content*, except when working together on a group project, but even then, it is clear that they are there to throw together, as efficiently as possible, a PowerPoint that will appease the professor. Is there no space for actual thinking outside the classroom, even at an institution of higher learning? Is it only possible as a performance? One of my pedagogy professors said an interesting thing once: teachers spend their time in the classroom teaching, while students, who you'd hope would spend the time learning, are actually *studenting*; that is, performing the gestures they've been taught to perform to seem like legitimate students. If you were ever a student, you probably know what studenting looks like: you ask a carefully crafted question that gives the impression that you've not been shopping for shoes online for the last twenty minutes, you nod now and then to seem enthralled, you laugh when you're supposed to, and you type loudly and frantically, which sounds like note taking rather than the chatting that it is. Universities today facilitate studenting more than learning. Another former adviser of mine thinks that universities shouldn't be organized by classes or disciplines but by projects; I think the word "project" appeals to him because it borrows the language of the office and sounds convincing to wealthy benefactors who've made their money in the business world. In the beginning, universities modeled themselves after cathedrals. Now, they feel more and more like expanding cubicles. Deep thought will be eternally at odds with this bureaucracy; they simply want different things. If many have begun to sense impending doom for the university as we know it, that is because two antithetical ideas have been forced into the same enclosed space with no pressure valve. The contemporary classroom invites online browsing during class and the proliferation of hopeless PowerPoint presentations. Walk between tables in any university library and you will see more people looking at Facebook than reading a book. (There's really nothing bookish about Facebook . . . it is all Face, no Book.) College is now where you go to network and to fulfill requirements. The classroom had always been a fine venue for acquiring knowledge, but now that it has been transformed into the same kind of room where conference calls happen, it's essential to create a serious and intimate environment elsewhere so that ideas can incubate. Some universities encourage faculty to eat lunch with their students or invite them for coffee, but these are more novelty outings than a permanent restructuring of the institution, something like a pizza party in elementary school. Perhaps I should invite the class to my apartment to gather around the keyboard, where we can put Rimbaud's "Le Bateau ivre" to music. (The thought is tragically appealing—appealing because it would totally work, tragic because it can never happen; student life has been cordoned off from real life.) A small detail, like a serious gathering space at the heart of the institution, could change the nature of conversations and get people to stop thinking like managers. You don't have to put on your earning face yet. "There will be time, there will be time / To prepare a face to meet the faces that you meet." Postpone the endless string of future meetings that await you. There is no need to rush into the arms of your future boss.

I can't help but think that there is a tiny wellspring in the soul of each undergrad that has been corked up by careerism. A distinguished French medievalist told me today, over hot tea in a grey corner, that the tipping point will be when students begin to turn down Yale to go to Deep Springs, the isolated and self-governed California college where students work on its ranch and farm and prepare meals in addition to their studies. He and I both think that the cork in the undergrad heart is removable. Since universities can no longer promise that "diploma equals job," maybe they'll be forced to return to a more noble mission than career prep. Some students pay tens of thousands of dollars in tuition, only to end up jobless after the four years of bureaucratic toil and without having acquired the fundamental life stuff anywhere. Anybody on board for recalibrating our priorities? Shall we pluck out the cork together?

A person reading this who has a full-time job, or several jobs, or a life of worries might be thinking, "All of these suggestions are made by and for someone with the luxury of time and energy to spare. How am I supposed to enter into this conversation when exhaustion is the primary feature of my free time?" Not everyone can commit a whole life to the study and practice of literature, music, art, or meditative thought. In high school, time was perhaps more abundant, which allowed us to listen to music without pressure and to ruminate alone in our rooms. We weren't adults yet, so we didn't have to worry about taxes or debt or rent. We were more invested in our sentimental lives because they took up the biggest amount of space in daily existence. Now, maybe with children running around the house and medical bills due and e-mails to answer and deadlines to meet and other practical matters—not to mention the yellowish shadow cast on our day by the media—aesthetic reflections are off the radar. But I have to insist on something: to allow the aesthetic aspects of life to be clouded out by chore living is to forfeit life itself. Some of the most beautiful things on the planet were made or consciously studied by people who were just barely getting by. Working and contemplating are not mutually exclusive; in fact, turning kids, bills, e-mails, and deadlines into occasions for reflection about life means joining centuries of attentive people who have realized that actual experiences of the everyday are the best place to look for insights about the human spirit. We haven't heard much of a poetic voice from the cubicle dweller, yet the cubicle is one of the most common forms of existence in the United States. Why is Kafka still the greatest bard of bureaucracy when so many know what it's like to get caught up in the cogs of administration? Depictions of work life often come from those on the outside looking in, but what if an assembly line worker told the story herself? Or a CEO? Or a bank teller, student, or barista? This could be one reason people feel alienated: because the most common experiences rarely get *deeply looked at*. Some think the only true material for art is love and death and birth and the other big cosmic stuff, but every inch of every day contains something interesting in it. Would it be so taxing to leave a pad of paper next to your desk and write down thoughts as they arrive? What about skipping the nightly news to listen to an album from start to finish, without doing anything else? Or walking down a street where you've never been or drawing the erratic contours of a crumpled piece of paper or sitting for five minutes on a bench and noticing sounds that arrive and depart?

My point is that poetry shouldn't be left just to poets, art to artists, music to musicians, philosophy to philosophers. I've always wondered why people so readily surrender these fundamental things, gladly handing them over to professionals. Why the will to self-ostracize from the world of thought and creation? Why this faith in a cult of experts when it comes to these few things owned by everybody? The amateur is an apologizer. In our all-or-nothing culture, you have to be a trained concert pianist or you should never touch a keyboard.

Or you have to do absolutely everything simultaneously, becoming a jack of all trades, master of none. Why the pardon-seeking tone in people without a music degree when they say, "I used to play piano a little, but not very well," as though the keyboard is a holy thing? It makes sense not to operate on someone if you're not a doctor; it doesn't make sense to give up drawing for lack of a graphic design degree.

In short, a life of consumption with no creation is a pointless life. The Other Serious makes more than it consumes and tries to get people comfortable with the idea that there is no monopoly on beauty and thought. Even worse than the cynicism and anger that loiter today in America is the more tragic fact that beauty and thought have been symbolically hoarded and rebranded as the property of specialists. People have begun to believe all the voices that tell them to just stay busy and consume more stuff, a safe activity that keeps them from thinking about the dangerous, essential questions elicited by literature, philosophy, and art: "Are we being our best as humans? To whom am I really accountable? At what point is refusal the best answer? Have I ever done a truly beautiful thing? Have I ever really said what I meant? What constitutes responsible thought, speech, and action?" Instead, people are supported in their self-absorption and centripetal thinking by undetectable, numbing forces. Individuals see themselves as the unique center of all things, not realizing they've simply become volunteer particles of a market demographic. Standardized uniqueness. Uniform individuality. To really do things differently makes one freakish. (Not the sanctioned kind of freakish, the bad kind of freakish.) I'm still on board with Emerson: "Trust thyself: every heart vibrates to that iron string." Revisit his self-reliance essay and you'll see that he's not talking about survival or self-sufficiency or freeing the self from societal dependency. He wants people to join the world by developing their own clearheaded conception of it. From one generation to the next, his idea never expires. He's talking to *you specifically*.

What the Other Serious proposes is simple, really. It gives language to a sentiment that is already there today in the minds of the conscious ones. You are by birth a card-carrying member of civilization and are thus responsible for it. No one really wants you to know this; things would be easier if you'd just passively accept your assigned role as a low-standards consumer, a human Pac-Man stuffing your face with pixels. There are other ways to go about life, like being three notches smarter than you thought you were and investing everything you do with aesthetic sensitivity. Wrest yourself from the dumb mesh of Web-informed living. Build an extra-reticular brain, that is, a consciousness that has escaped the net. Make your kid self and your elderly self pleased to be extensions of you. Write it all down, but keep most of it a secret. Go about the whole thing steadfastly, seriously, and with total elation at this, your one chance.

Postscript: The Lightness
of the Ladybug

While this book was in preparation, my grandfather passed away. Losing him was my first experience of real loss. I don't mean that this was my first experience with death; one by one over the years, I have lost grandparents and great-grandparents I am very fortunate to have known. I'm also familiar with the ruptures brought about by breakups, moving far away, and saying good-bye to friends and family and consoling landscapes. When I say that losing my grandpa in the summer of 2013 was my first experience of real loss, I mean that it was the first time I understood plainly the irrevocable absence brought about by the end of life. In the thirty-five years that he and I shared this planet, I could hear his voice anytime I wanted on the telephone or, even better, I could walk in his front door—it was never locked—and be greeted by his gentleness. Both of these possibilities have expired. It still says "Grandma and Grandpa" in my phone, but when I touch that number, he will never answer again. He was there, and now he isn't. It is no abstraction. I am starting to forget what his clothes smelled like when I would hug him.

I have a few indexical remnants of him, like some photos and a video I made a few years back, of him and my grandma telling stories about their lives. In the video, I asked him if he had any advice about relationships—I was in a tough one at that point—and he said, "Well, Christy. I guess I always just figured there is nothing worth getting upset about." I can't bring myself to watch the video again, but I always remembered this piece of advice. He's right, you know. Living in fret, worry, regret, anger, disappointment, and sadness simply accelerates your pace toward the end, clouding out all the beauty. Clinging to all of this stuff is like going through the most beautiful novels ever written and blacking out all the uplifting passages with a Sharpie marker.

Thoughts about him lead me often to think of the discrepancy between the kind of world that was his and the kind that is mine and yours. It is a relief to think that he won't have to bear the worst that is to come. He won't have to read about more shootings, more torture, more hate, and all the awful things people do to each other. No more new technologies for obliteration, no more bad blood. Still, I can't help but think that the planet was better while he inhabited it. His philosophy and his presence were moorings in a world adrift, at least for me.

My grandpa was a true Renaissance man. He knew how to fix cars, how to build houses; he knew everything about plumbing and electricity. He had worked in a candy factory and a leather factory. When he needed a special tool for a project he was working on, he would simply make one. His workshop is a museum of his improvisations, full of evidence of a resourceful and flexible mind. My grandpa was a quiet man who had mastered the art of joke telling; his eyes twinkled when he saw everyone in the family doubled over with laughter at his perfectly timed one-liner. He knew how to imitate many different species of birds by whistling; down in the pasture, you could hear him whistling a cheerful tune or the sparrow's song. His patience was infinite, his attitude kind. He provided for my grandma and five children, and became an unparalleled grandpa and great-grandpa. He never had one enemy in his whole life. He was joyfully serious.

In thinking about heaviness and lightness in America, I realize how much heavier his life was than mine. He spent his early years on a farm, and when his family didn't grow enough, they ate less. The arithmetic was very simple. You didn't argue or negotiate with it. The logic of survival was heavy and sturdy, like the tractor. There was no bureaucratic intervention between work and what was on the table. The abstraction we know today called a paycheck—a paper symbol of our work—played no role in that kind of life. Our paychecks aren't even paper anymore. They are diaphanous abstractions floating in non-space, the only connections between the work we do and the fact of our survival. Can we even be sure our paychecks exist? Are we sure of our own existence?

After he passed away, I was visited on several occasions by ladybugs. On the train in Berlin, as I was riding to the airport to go to his funeral, a ladybug landed on the window right next to my face and stayed there. At the visitation in Texas,

I sat outside the funeral home by myself in the warm air as a June storm rolled in and a ladybug landed on my hand. I wanted to show it to my grandma, to show her that grandpa was sending a sign he was okay, but it flew away before I got back inside. When I returned to Berlin, I was sitting on a balcony in Neukölln with my best friend and a ladybug landed on the wall above her head just for a moment and then flew away again. In the months that followed, ladybugs chose me over and over again as a landing spot. They found me indoors and outdoors. I asked people I knew if they'd seen more ladybugs that year, but no one had noticed any. I can't accept any other possibilities: either ladybugs are sensitive to sadness or they were sent by my grandpa.

The ladybug is a living button of lightness. In all the heaviness I felt in those first days of his passing, this little insect single-handedly picked up a grown woman. Each of its visits forced me to remember that death is only possible because of life. Heaviness and lightness are inseparable. This is why I think it is possible, even necessary, to be both serious and full of gratitude and gladness in every waking moment. Life can have mass without the downward heft of troubled thought.

This book—like my grandpa, like you and me—will be filed away eventually in a cosmic folder marked "Ephemera." In it, I've tried to think through what bothers me about living in a place that wants desperately to be light but that has so many varieties of heaviness it never figured out how to carry. I don't know whether people are naturally inclined toward goodness or badness, toward lightness or heaviness; each time I've felt sure of an answer, something came along to push me toward the opposite conclusion. It is unthinkable that we have managed *to exist*. The odds are all against it. But here we are, sharing the lot of anyone or anything that lives. The ant doesn't seem bothered by heaviness. Lightness doesn't bother the ladybug. They simply proceed, impartially. This is what I like most about life. It just proceeds, impartially. I may project joyful seriousness onto this procession in order to feel closer to it, but it doesn't matter. Life is indifferent to my projections. It doesn't care whether I like it or not. There's something flawless about this fact.

So, like a music box that labors out its last notes, articulated ever more slowly and roundly, I say a reluctant, definitive good-bye to my grandpa here and now. I accept living in a world without him, even though it is less good. The ladybug stays light no matter how heavy humans make things; my grandpa must have known this. I'll do what I can to keep my seriousness joyful, as a promise to him.

About the Author

CHRISTY WAMPOLE is an assistant professor of French at Princeton University and a member of Generation X. Originally from North Texas, she earned her Ph.D. from Stanford, and resides full-time in New Jersey and part-time in Berlin.